BREAKING
THE
MOULD

Or

Señor Schmidt

And Other True Stories About Ordinary
People Becoming Powerful.

Peter A Hunter

Librario

Published by

Librario Publishing Ltd.

ISBN No: 1-904440-43-6

Copies can be ordered from retail
or via the internet at:
www.librario.com

or from:

Brough House
Milton Brodie
Kinloss
Moray
IV36 2UA
Tel / Fax: 01343 850617

Printed in Times (11pt)

Cover design and layout by Steven James
www.chimeracreations.co.uk

Printed and bound by
DigiSource (GB) Ltd.

Revised Edition.

*This book is dedicated to
my wife Anne, without whom
nothing would have changed.*

Repression is at its worst when there is no complaint.

Jung Chang, Wild Swans

1991

Contents

Acknowledgements

Foreword

Backword

Glossary

Acknowledgements

These stories are an amalgam of experiences. They come from the personal involvement of all the people who contributed their practical experiences to make the stories live and all the people whose publications provided the basis for the models that allowed those stories to happen.

These include in no particular order :

Señor Schmidt for the patience, wisdom and the imagination that he demonstrated to allow the events that are recounted in the first half of the book to happen.

Aubrey C Daniels	"Bringing out the Best in People"
Stephen R Covey	"The Seven Habits of Highly Effective People"
Jack Stack	"The Great Game of Business"
Ken Blanchard, John P Carlos and **Alan Randolph**	"Empowerment takes more than a Minute"
Dr Spencer Johnson	"Who moved my Cheese"
Myles Downey	"Effective Coaching"

Also to **Connie Arsenault** of Snowy Owl Tours for her amazing perception.

The biggest acknowledgement is to all the Roughnecks and Roustabouts from the North Sea to South America whose stories, by being told here may allow others to understand the power of ordinary people.

Foreword

Breaking the Mould is an extraordinary performance improvement process. It is unique in that it does not use surveys, questionnaires, systems analysis or models for strategic change.

It sets out to change attitudes and relationships in the workplace. It does not set out to change the organisation or the structure of the business, neither does it rationalise or downsize.

These experiences, which are Breaking The Mould, have been documented and developed into a performance improvement process which is easily adaptable to any work situation, be it on the shop floor or in the office.

The stories are about the power of ordinary people when they are allowed to become powerful.

Breaking the Mould is what has to happen to make that change.

Most people want to do a good job, and want to be able to take pride in their work. When they don't do a good job it is normally because they are being denied the support, the materials or the feedback that they need.

These are stories about what happens when people are allowed to become as good as they can be, when people stop telling them what to do and start to give them the tools they need to become powerful.

These tools are Support, Encouragement, Respect.

The stories concern themselves with events on Drilling Rigs in South America and the North Sea. They tell of what occurred to allow the crews to take ownership of their work and some of the extraordinary performances which occurred when the old mould was broken. An eight-hundred percent performance improvement on one rig in three weeks was recorded, that new level of performance was then sustained. There are accounts of how semi literate, inexperienced crews in the South American jungle were taken from the performance you would expect from them, to a sustained world record in only two months; of roughnecks in the North Sea saving their company 27% (£3.9 million) of their operating budget in a single year. This book tells how these changes happened and how the same astonishing levels of performance are available for everybody wherever they work or live.

It is about people first and last and how to give them what they need to become extraordinary.

Involvement of the workforce is normally acknowledged as a vital ingredient in the success or failure of most management driven changes or initiatives, whether it is keeping the work site tidy, discovering efficiencies in a production process or implementing a safety programme.

In each case we only truly succeed in improving performance if we generate a change in behaviour that sustains the change in performance in the long term. To do this the work force must become involved, and in order to become involved there has to be something in it for them. Nobody will change their behaviour unless they experience a "Win" when they make a change.

There are many incentive and bonus schemes which work well in the short term. The reward however soon becomes an expectation and loses its power to act as an incentive. We humans as a species are fiendishly adept at defeating these engineered solutions with strategies which will allow us to continue to gather the reward without changing our behaviour.

The reward which cannot be bought costs nothing.

Imagine your department is due for a business review and you are well ahead of the curve with your preparation. On Friday afternoon it is announced that the directors of the parent company will be in the country and the review will now take place on Tuesday instead of the following Friday, to allow them to be present.

Your boss asks you to bring your schedule forward, this requires you to work all weekend to be ready.

Your efforts allow you to make the presentation on time and you are relieved that the directors do not appear displeased.

This is a familiar story of response to a pressure that is both difficult to resist and increasingly expected.

Now one of the directors walks across as you are packing away and says, "I'm sorry I couldn't rearrange my schedule to fit in with your original programme, thanks for your presentation, that was impressive."

Now, how do you feel?

The effort to give that feedback cost the director a few seconds of his time but the result is that now you can leap tall buildings.

Feedback which is Appropriate, Positive and Timely costs nothing.

Involvement is not an instant concept which can be bought. It has to be built up slowly and is the result of repeated experience.

Practising feedback within the team on all sides makes each member of the team become more involved. With time, confidence in their value within the team will increase and individuals begin spontaneously to produce ideas and suggestions because they know their opinion will be listened to and respected.

This level of involvement is not a trick. It is the result of a long-term change in the behaviour of the whole team.

How this change in behaviour is achieved is the real story.

Who it affects is the real audience.

Chapter 1
Meeting Señor Schmidt

I was a performance coach working for a company of Management Consultants based in Aberdeen, Scotland, and had just finished four months working on a semi submersible drilling platform on the very edge of the continental shelf in the North Atlantic to the West of Shetland. I was filling in for a colleague who had started the project twelve months before but had been forced to leave when another company made him an offer he couldn't refuse, more money. The original contract was not to be renewed so my job was to be a billed bum on a seat for the last two trips while the project wound down.

The winter had been severe in that part of the Atlantic where severe was the normal description for the weather in summer. It had been a difficult trip so I wasn't too upset when I was able to board the helicopter for the last time and wave goodbye to the rig.

Home at the beginning of December, I put my feet up and waited for news of the next project, hoping all the time that nobody would have any emergencies until after Hogmanay. There is still something special about the West coast of Scotland at New Year that cannot be bought or bottled, although there are a number of distilleries that get very close.

I received a call in the first week of January from my office in Aberdeen and after a very rapid run through the New Year's greetings I was asked if I wanted to go back to Venezuela. I had been to Venezuela several times before but was curious to learn a little more about the project before I committed myself.

This time the job was for a drilling contractor. I would be working a new oil field in the centre of the country away from the traditional fields in the West. The client was a partnership between a French Oil Company and the National Oil Corporation of Venezuela.

The country manager for the drilling contractor had six drilling rigs in the country. Five were in the West and had been on hire for many years. The sixth had arrived in the country six months ago specifically to work the new field.

The rig was drilling wells which went down to around a thousand feet then turned horizontally to drill along the thin oil bearing sand layer. The oil was thick and heavy and flowed very slowly. To create the production levels required the rig would drill up to twenty-four wells in each location, moving the rig about fifteen metres between each well. When the wells were completed the production would all be brought together at the surface in a single large manifold.

At a business review shortly after Christmas the South American partners had told the drilling contractor, rather unsympathetically, that if they did not achieve a radical change in their performance then they could pack the rig up and ship it back to where they had come from.

The country manager had not been expecting this reaction and for a while was at a loss, he had been doing his best and did not know what he could do to improve.

He remembered hearing of the work that I had done in Europe in similar situations and although for this size of operation I was going to be expensive, he was growing very short of cards to play.

My job was to go to Venezuela and turn around the performance of the rig. That phone call was the first of two. Did I want to go? The second call a week later was to tell me where to get my tickets.

I was lucky that I had to pack in a hurry because in retrospect, if I had considered everything that I didn't know about the project, where I was going, what I was going to do, where I was going to stay, what I was going to eat, I would never have been able to lift my bags for all the contingencies for which I would have packed. As it was, the only extra item I packed was a mosquito net. The altitude of the site and the lack of standing water meant that I never heard a single mosquito in the four months I was there, but it was still a comfort to have as I travelled out for the first time.

Meeting Señor Schmidt

The country manager who met me in the capital, Caracas, was an Austrian emigré called Gunter and was the man who had control of all the rigs in the country. I was taken initially to the company offices in Maracaibo where the nature of their problem was explained to me. In short the rig was on a warning from the client, who was quite capable of forcing them to pack up and remove it from the country. There was no deadline at the moment but in South America that simply meant that it could happen tomorrow. The meeting was relaxed but there was an image in my mind of the drilling company tied to the table with a Damocleasian sword coming closer to the jugular with every swing.

Gunter had done his research and in me he knew what he was getting. He was aware of the necessarily long term nature of my work and was reluctant to press too hard for promises of short term savings which he knew would be just that, promises. However Gunter still needed something to take away from the meeting to justify the extra expenditure to his bosses in Europe. I was very aware of the politics and asked Gunter what he was looking for. "What would really impress him?" Gunter's answer was "An improvement in casing running times."

Running casing was the last operation the drilling team carried out before the rig was skidded across the site - with hydraulic rams - to the next well. After the well had been drilled the casing would be run all the way to the bottom and cemented in place to stop the drilled hole from collapsing. When the rig left the site another smaller rig would arrive and prepare the well for oil production. Without the casing in place the hole would very likely collapse making it unlikely that the production tubing would be able to get to the bottom.

The casing was run into the hole in nine metre lengths. The actual time that it took to run the casing was not a large percentage of the total time on the well, but there was some pressure to run it as quickly as possible to minimise the amount of time that the formation was open without the protection that the casing gave it. If the hole did collapse before the casing was in place the consequences were serious. The casing already run would have to be pulled back to the surface and the drilling bit run again to clean out the collapsed section.

Gunter told me that the fastest the rig had ever managed to run casing was sixteen joints per hour. They would be impressed if the rig managed twenty joints per hour, a twenty five percent improvement. I pushed a little harder. What would really knock his socks off? What was the best performance ever? Gunter paused and looked towards Duncan his deputy, They conferred quietly for a second then Duncan spoke up and said that he thought the best ever, to his knowledge, was twenty five joints per hour. He thought that one of his other rigs had once achieved twenty five joints per hour in Europe but that you could hardly use something which had happened once years ago in a different country as a target.

Assuring him that I was not setting targets for anyone, but was just curious to learn what was the best, I could tell I had gone too far. Gunter and Duncan were no longer taking me seriously so I wrote down "Twenty five joints per hour," then closed my notebook and asked if there was anything else I needed to know or they wanted to tell me.

I flew back to Caracas the same afternoon and the following day was on my way to El Tigre, a town about two hundred kilometres north of the Rio Orinoco in the centre of Venezuela.

I was accompanied by Duncan, the deputy country manager, whose job was to introduce me to the rig manager, a naturalised Venezuelan called Willie Schmidt.

We met Señor Schmidt in his office in El Tigre where he rose to his impressive height of six feet four and took my outstretched hand with a dignified restraint. From what Duncan was saying it was obvious that Señor Schmidt had never heard of the process of "Breaking the Mould" and would have thought the image of a management consultant working on an oil rig rather humorous, if it had been happening to someone else. Clearly he was not amused that it was happening to him. Duncan sensed the resistance too and felt that he had to get me off on the right foot by selling the idea of what I was going to do for Señor Schmidt.

As the human race matures each subsequent generation seems to develop a greater resistance to salesmen. Watching Duncan, even with the

18

authority of his position as deputy country manager, I could feel Señor Schmidt's defences rising higher and higher. His expressionless face eloquently said that if Duncan were not his boss he would not even be in the same room with me.

I was trying to figure out what I could do to limit the damage that Duncan was doing. The more defensive Señor Schmidt became, the more work it would take for me to get him back on board later.

At that moment we were interrupted by Santa ("Saint" in English), Señor Schmidt's secretary, who had an urgent call from the rig. Señor Schmidt was torn between answering the call and continuing to listen to his boss. While he clearly wanted to embrace the former he felt obliged to do the latter. He was not going to be happy so I took the opportunity of suggesting that Duncan and I should go and find a cup of coffee while Señor Schmidt talked to the rig in peace. Duncan looked askance but said nothing.

We followed Santa who showed us to the kitchen then left us alone. I started to pour the coffee but could feel Duncan's impatience behind my back. I took my time with the coffee and when I was finished I turned slowly to offer Duncan the first cup. Keeping my eyes down and focusing on the cup, I turned back to pick my own cup up from the table, waiting for Duncan to speak. I turned slowly back to Duncan, bringing the cup up to my lips as I turned. He was going mad but held his peace until I couldn't keep a straight face any more. I smiled at Duncan who started smiling too, an automatic reaction, but he was still puzzled about what was amusing me.

I thought it was time to put Duncan out of his misery so I asked him what his job was. He replied that he was the "deputy country manager". I asked again, what was his job. "What do you do from day to day?" I said. Duncan thought a bit longer then he broke out into a real grin and said, "What you are really trying to say is that I am not very good as a salesman."

" Exactly" I said, "You've got it in one."

Duncan smiled then stopped and looked a little troubled. He asked me, "Where do we go from here? Willie is not very happy about what he is being asked to do. How will we manage that situation?"

"Don't worry," I said, "I think you'll find that that is my job".

I suggested a beer so we finished our coffees and set about winkling Señor Schmidt out of his office and down to the restaurant of his choice. He went home first and collected his wife, a charming Venezuelan whose calming influence probably went a long way towards making sure that we were up early and fit for business the next day.

Duncan had to catch the early flight back to Caracas and was feeling a little nervous that we had not spoken a word about business since coffee the previous afternoon, I assured him that the ball was rolling and I would see him again in three weeks when I came back from the rig.

Señor Schmidt was quiet on the way out to the airport and after seeing Duncan off drove back to the centre of El Tigre. He turned left at the traffic lights instead of going straight on, and as easy as that, we were on our way to the jungle.

I thought about how the trip had gone so far. The most important man at this moment was Señor Schmidt and he was not happy. He was the man who was responsible for the performance of the rig, and his behaviour and the things he said affected the way that the crews performed on the rig. Unless Señor Schmidt changed his approach and what he said to the crews, whatever happened while I was on the rig would stop the minute I left because Señor Schmidt's behaviour would drive performance right back to where it had been before I arrived.

My first challenge was to be able to talk to him.That might be difficult.

I had been sent to the rig without the people on it knowing anything about me or what I did. My time had been bought and paid for by the country manager without any reference to the rig.

This sent a message to Señor Schmidt that was loud and clear. "We are sending you this man to help because you are failing." For Señor Schmidt it was like a physical slap in the face. He had been doing the best that he could and now they were sending him someone who had never been on a rig before to help. It was insulting.

"How could someone who had never been on one of these rigs before manage it better than he who had been working these rigs for nearly ten years?"

He did not say anything but it was clear from his manner that he had received the message.

I knew that I had some work to do with Señor Schmidt.

From previous experience I knew that trying to sell an idea to someone in Señor Schmidt's position was the wrong thing to do.

As he said himself, he had been doing his best and to suggest that someone like me, a consultant with no experience of working on a land rig could do any better was insulting.

I knew that Señor Schmidt would not consider changing the way he behaved unless he could see value in making a change. This meant that I had to make the change first and then when he asked me how the change had happened, he would listen to what I had to say.

I knew how to be patient.

Diary Entry - The Best Of Times

Having worked in a variety of exotic locations I was in the habit of keeping a diary to record my slightly odd moments. This is an extract from the diary after one week in the Jungle :

"Venezuela is fine. It is the middle of the dry season and it has been raining for three days. The rain came through the roof of the box that I live in. When I switched on the bathroom light it blew up. In the box that I call my office the humidity is such that dry markers won't work. To get the atmosphere dry enough to be able to write on paper without tearing it I have to put the air conditioning on, but it is too cold with the air conditioning on so I keep the door open too. It is nice to sit in warm / cold damp / dry watching the rain. I had to go outside this afternoon. The hinge on my door broke and the door fell off into a puddle.

These are the best of times."

How easy in this situation would it have been to write, "These are the worst of times", and having written it, that is what they would have become.

Chapter 2

Willie Schmidt Owns A Car

The Venezuelan jungle to the South of El Tigre was not as lush or dense as I had expected, and the altitude meant that the air was a little cooler and the rains a little less frequent. In the southern summer it was pleasantly warm with a high cloud keeping off the worst of the sun and a pleasant breeze moving the air whenever the car stopped.

Señor Schmidt told me that it would take about three and a half hours to reach the rig so he settled down for the drive and I spent the time rubbernecking at the countryside.

It was difficult to characterise it at first because the land was dotted with the most twisted trees I had ever seen. They were at fairly regular intervals, about twenty to thirty feet apart, and they grew in every conceivable direction except up. They would start growing in one direction then suddenly shoot off in the opposite direction while sending a third branch in no direction in particular, as long as it wasn't related to either of the first two. No tree had a shape that remotely resembled any other. These were the only trees that were growing and I was amazed that the fences were held up with posts made from them. Since the trees were no more than two metres tall I could only assume that for each post a whole tree had been cut down. The more gross deformities had been removed with a chainsaw, then it was placed in a hole in the right position for the fence wire to be nailed to it. The result was not pretty but it worked.

The road was unusual for Venezuela, in that it was smooth with very few potholes. Señor Schmidt did not have to fling the pickup from side to side to avoid holes in the road, which he did have to do in town. This road had been laid by the oil company to service the new oil field, and had been built less than three years ago. The gentle undulations and lack of drama made it very difficult for me to stay awake.

I must have slept for an hour or more with my head on the window and was woken by the pickup oscillating from side to side quite violently.

Looking out I could see that we were crossing a river. As I woke up and looked around I could see that a large concrete slab had been laid across the bed of the river. The theory seemed to be that you just drive in and splash your way through. Señor Schmidt, seeing that I was awake was keen to explain that the rains had brought boulders down from the hills in the torrent and they were left on the ford when the river receded. They were only cleared if heavy transporters went through, and for the rest of the time everybody else just had to pick their way through.

Now that I was awake he was keen to engage me in conversation. Perhaps he was lonely driving on his own, or perhaps the complete lack of pressure from me had made him curious enough to try to find out more about what was going to happen on his rig.

He started by asking me where I had come from, how long had I been doing this kind of work, which other rigs had I worked on etc, until he had a good idea of my background without actually finding out what it was that I was going to do to his rig. Having got him this far I was reluctant to jeopardise progress by trying to sell him on something that he had not asked for. I decided to keep quiet a little longer until I thought that Willie Schmidt was ready to ask.

It is always difficult at the beginning of a project to say what is going to happen or how progress is going to be made because so much depends on what is needed or what is missing. Instead of making something up about what I was going to do I postponed the subject by asking Señor Schmidt about his own past.

I had expected a traditional oil industry background, which would normally involve a story about a shortage of funds in his early twenties which was going to be temporarily relieved by a summer job on the rigs. One summer stretches to two and pretty soon he is looking at retiring without ever figuring out what he was going to do after his summer on the rigs was over.

As usual when you take time to listen to people he surprised me with the variety of the work he had done in Venezuela and some of the insights he dropped into his conversation. He described one job he had in Caracas where he was the Regional Sales Manager for a large detergent company. There was a sales force of around thirty five, each of whom had a large imported car and spent most of the time tearing around the pot-holed roads chasing orders. Señor Schmidt was under pressure to reduce his transport costs, part of which amounted to a new car for each salesman every two years. At first it seemed impossible. After two years the cars were wrecked, and if anything they needed to be replaced even more frequently for the salesmen to continue to give a good impression to their clients. Señor Schmidt told me his idea.

When he had first arrived the cars had been leased and at the end of the two-year lease they were given back to the leasing company, almost worthless, in exchange for new ones. He suggested that instead of returning the cars to the leasing company at the end of two years, they continue paying for another year then give the car to the salesman.

I could see him glancing sideways as he drove, having told me this to test me and watching to see if I had understood.

I was impressed, and asked him if it had worked. It was obvious from the pride in his voice and the straightening of his back as he spoke that it had. He told me that the three years had been a bit of a sticking point at first because everybody still wanted a new car every two years, but when it was made clear that this was not going to happen slowly things started to change.

It is impossible to drive anywhere in Venezuela without the vehicle becoming covered in dust, and the further you go the worse it gets, yet when Señor Schmidt looked down at the company car park the cars were looking unusually clean. He started to notice little personal touches being added to the cars that had not been there before, here a Madonna on the dash board or a rosary hanging from the mirror, there some mud flaps, over there a chromed exhaust and that, he told me, was why he had done it.

At the end of three years the cars which were handed over to their new owners bore no resemblance to the two year old wrecks which had been previously given back to the leasing company. The cars which were given to the salesmen were accepted with pride and were driven away to begin another long life as a family car. The cost to the company was less due to the longer lease but the salesmen now took such care of their vehicles that at the end of their three years on the rough Venezuelan roads the majority still looked as if they had just come out of the showroom.

I asked Señor Schmidt what was the fastest car in the world. He said a Ferrari.

I told him no, it was a hire car.

Señor Schmidt told me to call him Willie.

I had used the analogy of the hire car in the past when trying to explain to people the concept of ownership. The word "Ownership" becomes a cliché which is bandied around as a sort of universal blame. "They just don't have any sense of ownership," is a frequently heard complaint about a workforce but it is said by someone with little idea of what the "Ownership" thing is that is missing or how to set about giving "It" to "Them".

I find it very refreshing to remind people of the difference in attitude which defines the difference between owning something and not owning it.

When you jump into a hire car the last thing you think about is washing it. We sit in the driver's seat, throw whatever we are carrying onto the back seat then have a quick check to make sure that all the parts to make it go are in the right place before twisting the key. We crash it into gear and with spinning wheels we fishtail out of the car park. Our clutch control may improve with use but our attitude does not. I knew from experience, as I had torn the bottom out of a beautiful silver Alfa Romeo which I had hired. It was on a mountain track in Sicily the previous summer and it had been less interesting to me than if the volume knob had come off the radio. It was not my car, I didn't own it.

When we buy a car, we first make a lot of decisions about it. What colour, what level of trim, what engine and any number of other variations that allow us to make that vehicle ours. Even with a second hand car we still decide which one is going to be ours and based on those decisions we become the owner.

We drive home carefully listening to the sound of it, we turn into the drive, emerging slowly so that everybody can see who the new car belongs to, then out comes the sponge and wax. Because this is our car we are going to take care of it, we own it.

Willie had taken his sales force from driving hire cars to driving their own cars and he knew the benefit to his company of the difference. I told Willie that what he had done was to create the conditions for what we called "Ownership". He told me what that meant in terms of pride and responsibility for the individual.

The warm breeze was having its effect on me again, and I could feel my eyelids growing heavy. Just before I gave up and went to sleep again I turned to Willie and told him what I was going to give to the rig crew.

I told him I was going to give them ownership of the rig, and as I settled down again I took a quick look across at Willie as he drove. He was smiling. I had a good feeling. He had understood and was on my side.

As my eyes closed I thought about this new relationship with Willie. My arrival in Venezuela had sent a huge negative message to him which was reinforced by the deputy country manager attempting to sell my process to him. Ordinarily this would have doomed any working relationship because Willie, already personally affronted by my presence was then being told by his boss to accept me.

Taking the pressure away was a deliberate strategy which had allowed Willie the space he needed to make up his own mind. Now by listening instead of talking I had discovered that Willie, in common with most other human beings, was a remarkable individual who, although he did not understand the buzzwords of Management Speak, did understand the changes that occurred when you gave people pride and self-respect.

That was a good start.

Diary Entry - The Mango

When I had been on the rig for a month I wrote in the diary :

"It is very warm now and we don't feel the weight of the pending rains yet. This is possibly because the Venezuelan weather forgot when the rainy season was supposed to be and dumped most of it on the rig last month.

Even in this heat I was a little surprised to see the night supervisor heading down the road when his shift finished with a towel over his shoulder. The nearest river is the Orinoco, which is over fifty kilometres away, a bit far for a morning dip. His purpose became clear when he returned an hour later with his towel bulging with mangoes he had picked in the jungle at the side of the road.

He gave me one.

It was not too big and had a scent like the flesh of a peach in summer. Heavy and firm it had just enough give to make your mouth water in anticipation.

The pleasure in postponing that first bite was incredible; I left the mango on the desk to tantalize me until lunchtime.

I am weak, I gave in. I sneaked back into my office in the middle of the morning hoping the mango wouldn't notice that I had broken my promise to allow it to live until lunchtime.

When I sat down I weighed it in my hand, rolling it slowly around to feel the flesh under the skin, deliciously playing with the moment when it would break.

Finally, that moment as my teeth with gentle pressure gained entry to the fruits gelatinous interior, I pursed

my lips and teasing the opening wider prepared for the
burst of taste.

The mango was rotten inside.

Now it is sitting accusingly on my desk like a large
pink mouse with one ear where I bit into it.

It seems to be saying. "If I was so good before, why did
you have to spoil things by biting into me?"

The answer to the mango's question has to be that if I had left things as
they were the badness would still have been there. The only difference,
like Shröedinger's cat, was that nobody would have known.

Chapter 3

Willie's Bet

We arrived at the rig shortly after midday. The last thirty minutes or so of the trip had completely disorientated me. We had crossed a number of rivers and been through innumerable crossroads taking apparently random choices between left, right and straight on. The jungle was also closing in and the terrain undulating so that the previously limitless horizon was now a lot closer. Apart from odd glimpses as we crested a rise there was nothing on which I could fix as a reference.

I saw one or two rigs through the trees on the way in but there was no sign of our rig until right at the last moment. Willie turned a wide sweeping bend going uphill and like a shock it suddenly appeared. There was no travelling towards the rig from afar, it was just there.

The rig sat on a two hundred metre by two hundred metre apron of concrete enclosed by a chain link fence with a huge and foreign derrick grinding noisily away in the middle. Willie stopped by the guard at the gate and after passing the time of day we were freed to drive onto the site.

As we drove in I noticed two rows of caravans which, Willie explained, were the offices and the accommodation. I saw that they were caravans in all respects except that they didn't have wheels, which strictly speaking made them boxes. The crew always liked to refer to them as caravans because talking about working and sleeping in a box was a little too close to the truth to be comfortable. At least by calling it a caravan they maintained the illusion that it was not a box.

The caravans were lined up in two rows against the fence and Willie proudly pointed to the one on the end, "This one we got specially for you," he said as he carried one of my bags towards it, "and that one over there is your office," pointing at another one exactly the same which had been parked about twenty metres away. The cabin had a single bed, a desk, a wardrobe and a bathroom. I was impressed but then I thought, "I always have been easily pleased."

Willie dropped my bag inside the door and told me to come with him to meet the German Toolpusher, Werner, who was a young man with perfect English and an antiseptic smile. Whatever he had heard about me, he didn't want it on his rig but while Señor Schmidt was there he was going to go through the motions.

The journey had taken a little longer than expected so after the briefest of introductions I was relieved when Werner suggested we get some lunch. I was relieved because Willie had started to do the same hard sell on Werner which Duncan had done on him, except that Werner had seen it coming and sidestepped towards lunch. Having moved away from the "Who are you?" and "Where have you been?" routine Werner got down to the nitty gritty of what concerned him. What did I want from the crews?

Willie looked worried because this was obviously a question that he had forgotten to ask.

I asked Werner if I could talk to each of the crews for an hour before the start of their next shift, somewhere away from the noise of the rig where they could talk. Werner pointed at the office box and I realised that instead of sharing someone else's office, this one had been brought in especially for me. A classroom in the jungle. I could see why Werner was edgy. He was supposed to be running a drilling rig not a school.

Werner explained that there were four crews who worked eight-hour shifts each. In any one day three crews would work. Each crew worked for six days then had two days off. I could talk to the first crew this afternoon, another this evening one in the morning and the last tomorrow afternoon, which would mean that I had seen them all in twenty-four hours.

I could see that Werner was not at all happy with the idea of stopping drilling for a meeting so I offered him a sweetener and said,"What about holding just two meetings, one at the shift change this afternoon and the other tomorrow morning, then all four crews could take part in half the time."

Werner nearly smiled, but not quite.

Willie was staying overnight so he would be on site for the afternoon and morning meetings. I thought that Willie and Werner could probably do with some time together before I started, I left them eating dessert and went to explore my new office.

The box was stuck on its own opposite the restaurant caravan and as far as I could see had no windows and only a single door. Werner had given me the key to the lock but as I opened the door, the handle fell off. This was ominous, this far away from the shops, if things broke the chances were that they would stay broken. The handle must have been broken during the move, and had split down the middle. I had managed to take the latch off the door before the handle came off so I went back into the restaurant box where I found a table knife. When I poked it between the door and the frame I managed to lever the door open. I took a rock from beside the chain link fence and put that in the doorway to stop the door from closing again. I hadn't realised how strong the sun had become until I was inside the office and took my sunglasses off. I had to wait several minutes while the interior faded into visibility. After some fumbling I found the light switch but realised that I would have to wait a few minutes more, the fluorescent tube remained obstinately dark.

The container was the same size as my sleeping box. There were two tables and half the room was taken up with white plastic garden chairs that must have been provided for the comfort of my expected pupils.

At the far end of the container was a large air conditioning unit high up in the end wall. Turning it on I realised that the lack of a door handle no longer mattered. At the rate at which the air conditioner was churning out icy air I would have to keep the door open to stop myself from freezing.

Feeling all round the unit I could find no way of controlling the temperature or the rate of the bone chilling blast, so it was either on or off.

A white board was set up at one end of the box with a selection of dry markers, black, blue, red and green. I thought briefly about their journey to get here, what crimes they had committed to deserve ending up here in a box in the jungle.

There was nothing else I could do for the moment but I wanted to give Willie and Werner as much time as possible together so I headed off to my sleeping box to unpack and try the lights.

The air conditioning was the same unit as the office with the same lack of control. By the time I had unpacked the room was beginning to feel distinctly chilly. I had to go outside again to warm up.

Outside I was met with the sight of the new crew milling around outside my office waiting for the crew that was coming down from the rig floor to get changed.

I noticed my rock on the ground, outside the closed door.

The rock had been placed carefully back in the same position I had left it, after the door had been shut.

Because the rock was stopping the door from closing I had left the key on my desk, inside.

I introduced myself to the crew and, guessing who the driller was, asked him where I could get the spare key. He made a gesture towards the Toolpusher's office. The gesture continued vaguely then ended up pointing to the sky. I took that to mean, "Maybe the Toolpusher has it but I haven't the foggiest idea really"

I knew that the container had only recently been delivered so I asked if anyone had been there when it arrived. One of the men, who it turned out was a translator/driver and therefore floated between the crews, said that he had been on site when it came and he thought that the key had been given to the Toolpusher. That counted as an almost definite" yes" so I went to the Toolpusher's office where Willie and Werner were having a chat over coffee. Werner had been watching my exchange with the crew, and when I explained the problem was quick to pull out a drawer full of keys. Werner himself had not been on the rig when the container arrived but he knew that if the key was anywhere it would be in this drawer. Fortunately most of the keys were labelled and after reading the labels I was able to discard most of them until there were only six single keys left in the drawer all without labels. Four of the keys were obviously padlock keys and they were nowhere near the right size, but the remaining two looked hopeful.

Returning to the container around which the crowd was now growing as the other shift changed and joined them, I tried the first key but no joy. It turned halfway then no further. I tried the second key and it would not even go in, I returned to the first key but now it would not turn at all. I could feel the crew pressing in behind. They had no idea that I had left the only key inside and were more eager than ever to get into the air-conditioned container. This was why the rock had been removed in the first place, so that it would be cold when they got in.

To most Europeans air-conditioning is a way of maintaining a comfortable temperature, and since we are not blessed with excessive heat its use is as often to heat the air as it is to cool it. It is therefore difficult to imagine the way that the Venezuelans, who are not far removed from the equator, use air conditioning.

I witnessed a very strange thing when I first went to work in Venezuela several years before. Working at a refinery in the east of the country near Puerto de La Cruz, I arrived for my first day in a short-sleeved shirt and headed for my office in the air-conditioned office building. When I went inside it felt like jumping into a cold shower, even after the short walk across the car park it was most invigorating. I found my office, the coffee machine, the people I had met before, the secretaries, the photocopier, the toilets, more people, and then made a quick dash to the toilets. On my first morning I was so busy meeting people that I barely got a chance to sit down. It was when I was in the toilet for the third time that I realised why. I had to keep going to the toilet because it was so cold. This sounds ridiculous considering how close I was to the equator but I was freezing cold and actually starting to shiver.

I left the toilet and went outside for a walk in the car park to warm up. It was as if on a cold night someone had just taken a duvet from the warm airing cupboard and wrapped it around my body. The air in the car park was thick and warm. It was heaven. I walked up and down for ten minutes while I warmed up but this time when I went back inside I no longer felt refreshed, just cold. I thought that if I, a Northern European, was feeling cold, how on earth did the Venezuelans feel? Then I realised that while I sat in my office in shirt sleeves and froze, all the Venezuelans were wearing heavy jackets, either padded bomber type jackets or thick leather. I later noticed that the jackets were all kept in the office. In the morning the Venezuelans would look forward to that first refreshing rush of air conditioning then go to their offices and put on their jackets in which they would then be comfortable for the rest of the day. I thought of the pleasure that the Scandinavians take in the excessive heat of the sauna. Perhaps the Venezuelans were taking the same sort of pleasure from the extreme cold provided by their brutal air-conditioning in comparison to the heat of the day.

I felt a little sorry for the crews who were looking forward to their reverse sauna in the container, I had no option but to explain to them what had happened. The crews helped me to one side and crowded round the door to offer their solutions. Werner stood next to me, and I could see that he was thinking hard while he watched what the crews were doing. They were concentrating on the lock and had inserted a knife blade between the door and the frame, applying all sorts of forces to the blade without result. I was sure that something was going to give suddenly and had visions of the broken blade sticking into someone's arm.

As I stepped forward to call a halt Werner put his hand on my shoulder and went forward himself to take control of the group around the door. He pointed at the hinges and as the serious faces turned to smiles, two men ran off. They went to a container next to the workshop and in less than a minute were back with a large hammer, a spike and a long screwdriver. The hinges didn't stand a chance. When the last one gave up the unequal fight the door stood drunkenly open. I was the last inside and found the crews fighting for the seats nearest the valuable air conditioner. Willie, Werner explained, would not be joining us.

He had said that he felt that his presence might either intimidate or inhibit the crew. I appreciated Willie's insight but had been hoping that he would be there as I knew that he had started to trust me, I still had not shown him the detail of what I was going to do with the crews or how I was going to do it. This would have been a good time.

I opened the meeting by telling the crews why I was there.

As I feel it is very important at this stage not to baffle people with concepts or jargon I told them I was here to implement the Continuous Improvement Process.

The Continuous Improvement Process is basically a method of capturing improvements every time a job is carried out. Each time a task is finished the crew get together and discuss what went well and what they could improve. These ideas are then captured and used to improve the performance next time.

The words translated well enough but in common with most people these guys had no idea what this meant in practical terms. How could you improve all the time? When would it stop? How much extra work will it cause me?

These crews had never seen or heard of performance coaches so at least I did not have to worry about any negative preconceptions. All I had to think about was how to let them understand enough about what was going to happen for them to take part.

At this point in a European project I would use a very simple story and explain the concept of Continuous Improvement.

When we buy our first car we usually spend all the money that we can afford and the result, although perfect in our eyes, is normally less than mechanically sound. Shortly after we drive home the exhaust falls off and we don't have much option other than to buy a new one and, with no spare cash, we fit it ourselves. The first time we attempt the job it takes all day, we lose most of the skin from our knuckles and the exhaust may or may not be gas tight when we have finished.

The next time the exhaust blows it will only take half a day to change it, we don't lose any skin from our knuckles and there is a good chance that the exhaust will work when we have finished. Without thinking about it we have learned which tools we need, how to use them and how the exhaust is supposed to be fitted. We have not learned all of the available lessons but we have captured a good deal in a natural process called gaining experience. We all do this all of the time.

One of the most valuable parts of gaining experience is that we have learned what not to do. The easiest way to improve is simply to identify what is not helping, then stop doing it. If we have lost the skin from our knuckles because the first time around the spanner slipped, next time we will definitely have the right size spanner, not only for this job but for any other job too.

That is the process of Continuous Improvement. In life it is called gaining experience and is an individual thing. In the work place however we are not dealing with one person performing one task. The next time the same task is performed it is highly likely that it will be performed by someone else. That person then has to make the same mistakes again in order that their own personal experience may grow. For everybody's experience level to grow they all have to make the same mistake. If when we make the mistake the first time everybody learns how to stop it happening again, that is clearly an improvement.

In this way when one member of the workforce learns something, every other person can make use of that same lesson.

I had been on a rig in the Northern North Sea which would drill a well every couple of months then skid the rig with hydraulic jacks over to a new well.

For practical mechanical reasons the wellheads are all separate at the surface. When drilling, the drill and the drill pipe go through the wellhead into the well. To start work on a new well the whole rig must be physically moved until it is vertically above the new wellhead.

There were four crews on this rig and every time it was skidded the crews would come together and talk through the operation they had just completed. They would identify things they could do better next time or things they didn't want to do next time. At each skid they would collect their ideas and record them. As they would then use those ideas the next time they skidded the rig to tell the crew what had been learned from previous skids, the next skid would be better. That was Continuous Improvement.

Having been on the rig for nearly a year I was winding down my involvement in the project and handing my position to a crewman who had been trained to take over. One of the last operations was to skid the rig to a new well. The assistant driller who was due to make the skid was worried and revealed that, through chance, it was actually two years since his crew had skidded the rig. They had a procedure but that didn't tell them "how" to skid the rig. I took the whole crew through all of the lessons that had been learned in the past year by the other crews. In effect they were given all the experience that the other three crews had gained from all the past skids.

There were a few questions of clarification and discussion but the crew left the meeting and skidded the rig perfectly. At the debriefing session they returned with lessons of their own. Their biggest lesson was the value they had found through making use of the knowledge which had been gathered by the other crews.

For the Venezuelans I knew that the broken exhaust analogy wouldn't work. When a Venezuelan buys a car, if it has an exhaust he will want to know why it is not making as much noise as his neighbours' car. He will most likely not buy the car until the seller has put a hole in the exhaust to make it sound normal. It does not say much for Venezuelan motoring but I knew it was true.

I had to look for a way to get the crews to understand what was happening without patronising them.

The best way of doing that, I thought, was to stop talking about it and start doing it. Instead of making them listen in an increasing temperature in a box in the middle of the jungle, I asked the crews to start talking. I asked them to tell me which one of all the operations that they carried out was the one that they disliked the most. Almost unanimously they agreed that it was skidding the rig.

On this site in the jungle it involved attaching large hydraulic jacks and pulling the whole rig from one wellhead to the next. The wells were fifteen metres apart and there were two dozen wellheads in two lines down one side of the concrete apron.

I wanted to start collecting the crew's ideas so I got my dry marker and wrote Delizando (skidding) at the top of the dry board. It didn't make a mark. I tried a different colour and still nothing. Another marker marked my finger but still wouldn't work on the board. When I felt the surface of the white board, it was wet.

The air conditioner was pouring cold dry air in at one end of the container and I was by the open door at the other end, right where the cold dry air met the warm wet air outside. I was standing with the board in a little cloud all of my own.

Lesson number one, a dry marker will not work on a wet board.

I couldn't close the door because there was no window, and the only light was coming from the open door. Werner came to the rescue again and suggested that we position the board at the other end of the container, the cold end, and the crew would have to come and sit in the cloud end.

This sounded like a good plan but the container was too crowded to move the wet dry board up to the other end. The crew were beginning to enjoy this so as soon as they saw the problem they all jumped up with their chairs and went outside into the sun while I picked up the board and went to the cold end of the container. Then they all filed back in again and sat down facing the other way.

The board had dried by the time everybody was back and I asked again which was the operation that they disliked the most. This time they shouted back together "Delizando", and I wrote Delizando at the top of the board. Next I asked them to tell me what they did that made them dislike the job. At first it was mostly directed against the European supervisors. "They shout at us all the time", "They don't give us any respect", "They are swearing at us all the time", "They are putting pressure on us which causes mistakes and makes more delays". All these general gripes were acknowledged and written down, then I found myself writing more and more task specific points.

"It takes a long time to get the generator if we have to do any welding."

"When the tractor goes away to pull the hydraulic unit we have to stop skidding because we need the tractor to lay the skid plates."

"We have to wait while the logging unit disconnect their remote sensors from the rig."

The ideas were coming thick and fast and I was running out of room to write them.

Werner found another whiteboard and gave me that. I was writing smaller and smaller but there was no let up, and I had to call a halt when I reached the bottom of the second column on the second board.

I explained to the crews that it was three days before they were going to skid the rig again. I would write out all the suggestions from these crews and add all of those from the other two crews and, before the next skidding operation, I would help the crews work out how they could incorporate them into the next plan. If the crews were happy I would take fifteen minutes of their time before each shift and work out as many ideas as possible. When they skidded next time each crew could use the ideas from all of the crews. Did that sound like a deal?

"Thanks for your time, I'll see you tomorrow," I said, and they wandered back out into the sun, some to get changed for work and the others to get on the bus for the three hour trip back to El Tigre.

While I sat on in the gloom the crews left and Werner came back in. I could see his head cocked slightly to one side and that he was thinking, "I could have done that." I waited and eventually Werner asked, "So that's it, you just ask them how to do their job then tell them to go and do it."

In a nutshell, I had to admit that was what I did. There was however one small exception that would make the difference between the crew changing the way they worked, or continuing to work the same way they always had. Nobody was going to tell them to do anything. The crews would decide what changes they wanted to make, and then they would implement those changes themselves.

This could have been a bit strong for some Toolpushers who might fear losing control but I knew from Willie that Werner was under a lot of pressure to make the rig pay. I was counting on him understanding that the more the crew could do for themselves the less strain it would be on him. This would allow him more time for the business of running the rig, instead of running the crew.

I had gambled with Werner on what he saw as control. For many managers "control" is the ability to tell people what to do. Telling people what to do does not necessarily achieve anything but for these people relinquishing control is frightening because they have no idea how else to spend their day. My observation of Werner was that telling people what to do was something he would rather not be doing, he just did not know another way to get people to do what he wanted. Werner was open enough to welcome my suggestion in a situation where other individuals may have seen it as undermining their authority and resisted vigorously.

I could see that it made sense to him but Werner had still not known me for more than six hours and was understandably cautious. "OK," Werner said, "we will only do this for the skidding operation and you let me know how you are progressing." I smiled a little to myself and said, "Of course Werner, you will always know what is going on."

As he walked back outside into the light I saw him bend down to pick something up outside the door. He brought it into the container and put it on the desk. It was a coffee percolator. He said with a straight face "If you are going to stay then you will probably need one of these. There's coffee and filter papers in the galley and they will give you a bottle of water too, don't use the stuff out of the taps it'll kill you. I'll be back for a cup when I've got the rig started again". Werner left the container and I set about producing the coffee.

I collected everything I needed from the galley and switched the coffee machine on. I had just plugged in the laptop when there was a knock on the door. I was going to say come in but a loud bang and a flood of light suggested that the door had had enough of being propped up and had fallen over. I got up and went to the door. Shading my eyes against the brightness of the sun I could see a young Indian boy standing looking at the fallen door absolutely horrified. He looked at me worriedly then back at the door, but I couldn't laugh. Instead with a serious face I showed the boy the hinges and the lock and explained the story about the key. The boy finally relaxed when he realised that he was not going to be blamed for breaking the door and he told me why he was there. He said with great pride, "I am Eduardo, assistant to the electrician."

Señor Werner had told him to come and change the light so he had brought a filament bulb. I was trying to explain to him the difference between a fluorescent strip and a normal bulb when Willie came in looking as if he was ready to steal Werner's inaugural cup of coffee. I wrote a note for Eduardo to take to the electrician and sent him off saying that the electrician would tell him about the different bulbs.

I poured the coffee for Willie hoping that Werner wouldn't be too upset to be missing the first cup, and gave him my impressions of the crew and how the first session had gone. Eventually Willie had to ask again, what was I going to do?

I asked him how long it had taken to skid the rig last time. He had been on site when they skidded two days ago, and said with some pride that it had taken six and a half hours, which was the fastest they had ever done it. Having listened to the first two crews' ideas I was prepared to take a gamble based on my belief in the power of ordinary people, and told

Willie that I was going to be on site for the next three weeks. I said, "At the end of those three weeks the crew will skid the rig in one hour. That is what I will do for you".

"Absolute rubbish," said Willie. He had been on site for the last skid, watching everybody running round like crazy, he had seen the Toolpusher shouting and tearing his hair out, and had seen the crew working flat out. There was no way. The more Willie talked the more I knew it was a sure thing.

I said, "Willie, I bet you one beer. One beer says that the rig will skid in one hour before I go home." He protested but I refused to be drawn into a discussion about the impossibility of the bet. Take it or leave it. Eventually I wore Willie down and we shook hands.

The bet was on.

I have always disliked the idea of selling. I have never consciously done it and always automatically resisted when it was done to me. This was my individual reaction to being told what to do by a salesman but I recognise that many other people have exactly the same reaction.

I liken this reaction to walking around a second hand car lot. You see the right car in the right colour at the right price and decide to buy it. After you have made your decision a salesman comes and starts to try and sell it to you. You will refuse to buy it on the grounds that if the salesman wants to sell it so badly there must be something wrong with it.

My answer when using the Breaking the Mould process, to avoid this defensive reaction, was not to sell at all. Instead like any shop I prefer to set out my wares and allow my customers to make their own minds up.

Using this approach with the crews avoided building resistance to change. I had not sold them the idea of Breaking the Mould, but instead I showed the crews how it worked and allowed them to make their own decisions.

I have a lot of faith in people when they were allowed to make up their own minds. This was the first time I had ever made a bet on it.

Diary Entry - The Frog

I did not keep up my diary on a daily basis. I used it more as an undemanding friend with whom I could share my experiences. One day I wrote :

"In my sleeping box last night I was woken in the small hours by a noise rather like a large fat drip, coming from the bathroom. That I should even notice such a noise was odd, perhaps it was the irregularity that held me wide-awake. I found myself fascinated, and puzzled because I could detect no pattern to the noises, each one like a large liquid 'plop' that held no water. I rolled over and reached for my torch (the light had become history during an unseasonable downpour).

I switched it on and I found myself staring at a small bright green tree frog, which was looking up at me rather quizzically and blinking in the unaccustomed light. We considered each other for a while and I decided that he would be welcome to stay to help me deal with ants and the other insects that occasionally also found their way in to the box. He wandered off under the bed in search of a light snack and I turned over and went back to sleep.

In the morning I couldn't find him but as I was shaving the now almost familiar "plop" came from behind me, and there he was looking up at me with his head half cocked to one side as if to say, what on earth are you doing? We chatted happily for a few minutes and I left for breakfast, flicking the air conditioner on as I left.

One thing always leads to another and it was not until 10:00 hrs that I returned to my cabin. The room was freezing and there in the middle of the floor in a shivering heap was my poor frog. I felt awful, so as carefully as I could I picked him up and put him outside

45

while I switched the air conditioning off and tried to warm up the room. He was barely moving so I left him in the sun while I went back to the office.

It was a busy morning and I didn't get back to check on him till lunchtime.

He was dead.

Sunstroke!"

Chapter 4

Breaking The Mould

I didn't talk to Willie any more about skidding the rig but over coffee I filled him in a little about where he personally fitted into the process, and what it was that the process expected of him.

I said that I would be collecting suggestions and ideas for improvement from the crew. Some of the suggestions could be dealt with on the rig but there would be some that would need his help to get implemented.

I explained that when I collected suggestions there were two effects that I looked for. The first was the obvious one of an improvement in the way in which the rig did its business, a change of equipment or a new procedure, but that there was another equally important effect, which was that the crew, by receiving feedback when they made a suggestion, knew that someone was valuing their opinion. They would know that someone was giving them respect and for the Venezuelan crews I knew that respect was more important than money. I asked Willie that, when presented with these suggestions he try his hardest to do what they suggested, even if the idea was not perfect. If he did have to say no, then when he did he must give an explanation why not.

Whatever the issue I asked that he never ignore an idea. To help him I would store all the lessons and ideas on a database. In this way even when he was busy I would help him to make sure that no suggestion or idea was ever forgotten. That was simple enough and Willie agreed.

As Willie was pouring his second cup of coffee Werner walked in.

I could see that Willie wanted to share the bet with Werner, either to get him on his side to ridicule the bet or to try to help me by setting it as a target for Werner. I did not want either to happen. I certainly did not want anyone taking sides at this early stage and I definitely did not want Werner to get the message that I had set a target for him. He would either accept the target and shout and rage at the crew even harder to try to achieve it, which was unlikely, more likely he would refuse to accept the imposed target and start to work to undermine the process.

The Breaking the Mould process is robust and can cope with uncommitted or negative people. If people don't understand enough to make a reasoned decision they will stand back and wait while the evidence unfolds. Each person will, at some point, become convinced by the evidence they see and will join the process. They become committed to the process because they have decided for themselves that it is the best thing to do. If people are told what to do they will stop doing it as soon as they are no longer being told. When they decide what to do for themselves the change is sustained and that is what makes patience so vital. Without the patience or faith to wait for the sustained change there is just lip service, which disappears the minute the implementer's back is turned.

The Breaking the Mould process focuses on creating the conditions for ownership then giving support to the individuals when they decide to take it.

Breaking the Mould can cope with people who are openly hostile to the process and make it their mission to undermine it. As long as the door is left open these people invariably come back when they see the benefits for themselves and become champions of the process. Sometimes it takes a huge act of faith to continue to believe this. My hardest nut to crack was a committed shouter and control freak working on a rig in the North Sea. It had taken over two years for this man to realise what was happening and embrace the process.

If at any time during that period I had stopped taking care of this man, if I had stopped providing him with information about the process, if I had stopped letting him see what was going on or taken any of his tantrums or his outbursts personally then I would have lost the man and he would have remained a bitter opponent. If that had happened it would have become his object in life to dismantle the process the minute I left the rig. As it was, that contract was a particularly long one and after two years when I was thinking for the umpteenth time what I could do to allow this guy to join in before I left the rig, I saw a strange thing.

Whenever a new face joined the team I always made a point of introducing myself and spending a few minutes explaining what was going on. Just enough to set the expectation about the routine of planning meetings and debriefs which had become a part of the way the rig did its business.

A new supervisor joined from a different rig and he was accustomed to being unquestioned in his authority and definitely in charge. He was a young man who had risen to his supervisor's position relatively quickly. I talked to him to set the expectation about the way the rig worked and what his contribution was expected to be to the overall process.

At first he seemed happy, but very soon he started to become irritated with having to tell everybody everything about what he was going to do or had to be done. He could not see the need to tell the night shift when he had already told the day shift and since he knew everything he could not see why he should have to ask anybody else's opinion. I was happy to let things ride, so that without pressure the supervisor could relax and perhaps look at things more clearly, but the new supervisor was not so patient, and after a week he went to the hard nut Toolpusher and asked him why he had to put up with all this "bull".

Normally the hard nut, when having a "private" conversation with an individual would slam the door to his office and have his private conversation in exactly the same way that an ostrich would, completely uninhibited and oblivious to the world because he could not see it.

This day he asked the supervisor into his office and did not shut the door. My desk was outside and along with everyone else in that outer office I listened while the Toolpusher explained to the new guy exactly what was going on and how he as a supervisor had a responsibility to his crew to be seen to be showing them the correct example.

The supervisor came out shell-shocked; he had gone in expecting sympathy and had come out after twenty minutes of an extremely hard conversation. I left the rig three months later secure in the knowledge that the process was in good hands.

The above is true, as the process will always allow people to come to it when they are ready but it is much harder work to swim against the tide and I for one, when presented with the option of working with someone or against would always select the easy way.

I had no wish to upset Werner, so before Willie could wreak his innocent damage I recapped for Werner's benefit exactly how he would see the process working day to day. I told him what I had explained to Willie. At the heart of the process were the suggestions and ideas that I was able to get from the crews about improvements they wanted to make to their jobs. These suggestions and lessons would be gathered as soon as practically possible after an operation was completed.

Lessons that involved a change in the hardware i.e. the machinery or tools would be dealt with by the Toolpusher or the superintendent by either saying yes, and purchasing the required equipment, or saying no and providing feedback to let the originator know that he was not being ignored. This feedback is the key to creating the conditions for ownership.

Lessons or ideas that involved changing the software, by which I mean the procedure or the way that an operation was carried out, would be dealt with on the rig. Ideas would be collected from the crews to use the next time they did the same job. Every time they did a job they would learn from it and the next time would be an even better implementation. This way the crew would always know more at the start of the next operation than they did the last time it was performed.

Two cups of coffee was enough. I felt as if I had been talking the whole day and I saw that as a bad sign in a business where it is so important to be able to listen, to find out what is important to your audience. Werner made his excuses and went up to the rig floor, Willie went with him. I put my feet up on the desk, turned off the air-conditioning and offered thanks to the continent that had invented the siesta.

Behind my closed his eyes I reflected that I had made significant progress with both Willie and Werner. Now they both knew the words that described the process and when they saw it in action I was confident that they would be able to fully understand and develop the power of their own contributions.

Diary Entry - The Blessings of God

As the project advanced I continued to record my thoughts about the crews. I noted that punctuality in South America was not a big issue. The word "punctual" translates into Spanish but it is not often used. One night the crew bus was later than usual and I wrote in my diary :

"When the rains finally broke in the jungle we were inundated on site. The drains were all full of the year's dust and jungle debris. They blocked solid with the first flood.

Tonight the crew had a small problem when their bus unexpectedly left the road. When the Venezuelan dust first gets wet the roads become very slippery until with time and more rain they are washed clean. The driver was taking particular care as he brought the crew in. Unfortunately the field production engineers chose the same night to lay their pipeline across the road. The planning for this event seemed to consist of doing it quickly while nobody was looking.

The engineers had dug a trench three feet deep across the road and were bringing up the pipes when our crew's bus appeared around a bend. To be fair the production engineers were probably as surprised as the driver, who naturally braked, and then continued in a straight line while the road continued to curve around to the left.

After a short trip through the country the bus came to rest up to its axles in the fresh mud that the pipeline crew had thoughtfully provided for them.

The first reaction of the crew was to jump out of the bus into the mud, in which they too soon became stuck. They could not get back to the bus or reach the road. The crew had to wait in the pouring rain up to their knees in mud until a bulldozer from the road crew was released to come and get them. It returned to extract the bus. When the crew and bus had been restored to each other, on the other side of the trench, they continued on their way to the rig, both covered in mud but none the worse for the experience. They arrived at the rig late and damp but in high spirits. The rain continues to cause problems, not the least of which is that the crew have to work in it, and yet, if it were possible, they seem to go about their work even more cheerfully.

I asked them why they were not bothered by the rain. They said how could they be bothered, the rain was "Las Benediciones de dios", "The Blessings of God."

Regardless of faith or outlook I found something very refreshing in this simple phrase.

Chapter 5

Willie's Cushions

After the meetings with all four of the crews I took stock of the mass of information I had received and found that I had collected a list of seventy-four suggestions for improvements to the skidding operation. These were either positive suggestions to improve the operation or simply ideas to stop doing things that wasted their time.

Over the next few days I went to their Charlas. (Literally translated it means a chat). They gave me fifteen minutes of their time before each shift and I used this time to ask them how they were going to make each of these suggestions happen.

Gradually the list of actions was completed and on the day of the first skid each of the points had been addressed. Finding that one action addressed several problems I had a list that totalled thirty two significant changes to the skidding operation.

I spoke to the crew who were going to carry out the operation, with the list of thirty two changes in my pocket.

I asked the crew if they felt ready for the skid, and was there anything else they could think of that would be a benefit to the operation.

"No," they said, they were ready and they were happy. This skid, with the work they had done, was going to be good.

I agreed with them, I told them to take their time to be safe, and I kept the list in my pocket.

At that moment the crew owned the answers to all of the improvements they wanted to make. If I told them to use the list I would in effect be telling them how to do their job. That would remove their ownership.

Good things come to he who waits.

I watched the skid without a notebook or a clipboard or a stopwatch. I spent my time wandering around talking to the crew about whatever they wanted to talk about. Someone would have a new idea, "Can we use the Company pickup to pull the power pack?" Someone else would be curious about Scotland, "Was it an island?" The crane driver wanted me to bring him some whisky next time he came out. I had to explain to him that a bottle of Scotch whisky was actually cheaper in Venezuela than Scotland, which was quite difficult to do.

The skid finished and Werner wrote in the log that it had taken five hours. That represented a significant improvement over the best ever time of six and a half hours but Werner was still puzzled. He knew what I had been doing. I had told him that the crew had worked out thirty two different ideas to improve the skid and he had seen some of those ideas being used. He was puzzled that the improvement was not more significant, but I asked him to wait and see what the crew said at the debriefing.

I debriefed the crew the following day at their next Charla. They were withdrawn, not at all the noisy animated group I had seen before, now they were very subdued and it was difficult to get them to speak.

They knew that they had skidded in five hours and they knew that the Gringo was going to shout at them for not doing it quicker because that was what always happened.

I asked them what they thought had gone well.

I shut up and waited. There was a lot of glancing backwards and forwards through lowered eyes and then the crane driver said that attaching the welding unit to the rig had been a good idea because he did not have to waste time lifting it to keep it up with the rig when it moved. There was a nervous silence. Now was he going to get shouted at? I wrote it down on the board and asked what else. In no time the room became animated again and the list of what went well began to grow.

It did not take long to fill half the board and then it began to slow down. Now I asked what did not go so well. I was off again scribbling to keep up with their ideas. I filled up the other side of the board. By this time the other crew would have been chafing to get away from the rig so I let the crew go to change for work and promised to continue next time. In the meantime I would ask the other crews how they would solve the problems. I made progress with the other crews but the breakthrough came the next time that I spoke to the first crew which had skidded the rig. By this time half the points on their list had been dealt with and removed, but the driller asked me to put up the original list again. I did so then gave him the pen and sat down with the crew. I knew what was coming and wished that Werner had been there to see it too.

When the driller stood up and went to the board, it felt like one of those moments when the world stops.

He stood in front of the board and read the list of things they could do better then started putting ticks against some of them. I could see which they were and could see where he was going with it. He then turned around and asked the crew if they could see why he had ticked the points he had. Nobody even guessed, and after allowing a pause I put my hand up.

"Are they all the same ideas which you had the first time I wrote out the list?" I said.

The penny dropped and suddenly everybody was blaming each other for forgetting to do what they had said they would do last time. I put my hand up again and the driller motioned for quiet. I told them that it didn't really matter who had forgotten, what mattered was how could they make sure that they did not forget again next time, or if another crew did the next skid, how could they make sure that the other crew did not forget.

The crane driver asked if I could make them a checklist to use so that they would not forget again. I said their checklist (which was still in my pocket) would be ready the next day, and if they thought it was good enough it could be given to the other crews too.

The following day Willie turned up. Because of the distance he only visited about once a week and despite the daily phone call he and Werner had a lot to talk about. I had spoken to Werner about the checklist and why it was still in my pocket during the first skid. I told Werner that since the first checklist had not been the crew's idea, giving it to them would have made the crew feel as if they were being told what to do even though the ideas were all their own. Now the checklist was not my list, it belonged to the crews and I was just the person who had the printer and could make the changes. This was the crew's checklist of their own improvements, they owned it, and because they owned it, they would use it.

I noticed something else which hadn't happened before. The crews were now asking what they could do while they were still drilling to prepare in advance for the skid

Now I was just their clerk. The crews were running the meetings.

I knew that Werner wanted to give me every chance to help the crews. I had no idea about the nature of his conversation with Willie that day but when I met Willie after lunch it was clear that progress towards improvement, or apparent lack of it, had been discussed at length. I felt there was little value in trying to defend the crew's performance so I pre-empted any criticism by reminding Willie of the promise he had made on the first day, which was that if I asked him to consider an idea, he had said that he would try his best to make it happen. If he couldn't make it happen then he would tell me why not so that I could feed those comments back to the crew. Raoul the assistant driller had given me a suggestion.

The previous day I had been waiting for the crew's bus to arrive. That was my excuse to spend a couple of minutes with the guard at the gate chewing the fat. The real reason was that I only had fifteen minutes with each crew before they went on shift and I didn't want to waste any of that time.

When the bus arrived, it was an eighteen-seater van and every crew change it brought eighteen people, often more.

The trip took three hours and I could only imagine how that must have felt cooped up pressed against each other in the heat in the van. On their arrival I would watch them emerging and they invariably spent several minutes bending and stretching to iron out the wrinkles caused by the journey.

On this day they piled out as usual and Raoul, after finishing his stretches, came over to talk to me. He asked if he had heard right at the introduction meeting when I had explained why I was there, that I wanted to know any ideas which would make the operation better. I said yes, I had deliberately used the word "better" instead of faster or more efficient and was pleased that Raoul had remembered.

I said, "Tell me your idea and I will see what can be done."

Raoul seemed a little embarrassed at first but once he started it poured out. His concern was about the bus. Raoul launched into a litany of problems: overcrowding, cramped conditions, omitting to pick people up, some men having to walk for an hour to the pickup points and the length of the journey itself. There was a whole raft of issues that he just wanted to tell someone, to get off his chest, but I realised that he was just setting the scene. None of this was his real point.

Finally he said it. All that Raoul wanted was cushions on the seats. The front seats, occupied by the driver and the driller were upholstered and they were fine, but the rest of the crew had to sit for three hours each way, to and from the rig on the jungle roads, on hard wooden benches.

Now I understood the reason for the elaborate stretching exercises that went on whenever the bus arrived.

I wrote down the idea in my notebook and promised to see what could be done.

Now I had Willie's attention, after reminding him of what he had promised, I told him that the first idea was, "Could we have some cushions in the bus?"

Willie did not explode but he came close to it.

"Cushions on the bus, Cushions! Where do you think you are? This is an oil rig! We are in the middle of the jungle! Do they think this is a holiday camp? What will they want next?"

I weathered the storm and after Willie ran out of steam I asked him what sort of ideas had he expected to get from the crews. He said that he was expecting ideas which would save money running the rig, ideas to speed up the operation, ideas to drill better wells, not cushions.

Then I asked Willie, "Suppose that Raoul had an idea tomorrow which cut your costs by ten thousand dollars a week. Is that the sort of idea you want?"

Willie didn't even think, saying,"Yes of course it is, I'm not running a charity".

I continued, "Do you think that Raoul would give you that ten thousand dollar idea tomorrow if today, when he asked for cushions he did not get them?"

It was a light bulb moment; Willie opened his mouth then stopped and looked at me through narrowed eyes. I could see him replaying the conversation and could see understanding flashing across his face. He started to smile and the next thing he said was, "What colour cushions should I get?"

I was starting to feel good about Willie. He had made the jump from the theory to the practical application. I knew that no matter how much I talked and explained about what was happening the only way that Willie would truly understand was when he worked it out for himself. In the same way that I had allowed the drilling team to figure out their need for a checklist, I had allowed Willie to work out for himself the value of his support for the crew. Now he understood that when he provided support for the crew they would in turn provide support for him.

Two weeks later, just before I left the rig to go back to Scotland the rig was skidded in fifty-five minutes. In three weeks the crews had made an eight-hundred percent improvement in the time it took to skid the rig.

I won my bet and Willie bought me the beer.

The crews now planned the skids and held their own debrief meetings to sustain their level of performance. They owned the operation and in the next four months the skid never again took more than one hour.

The most important thing was that Willie now asked me how I had done it. Before the dramatic improvement he would not have listened to any explanations or coaching because he could not see how it was going to work. Now he was asking me how I had made that change because he wanted to understand for himself what he could do to sustain it.

His request was vital for the sustainability of the project. Without Willie understanding and being able to create the same conditions for himself, his behaviour would drive the crews' performance right back to where it had been before I joined.

By responding to his request I was able to coach him and he was able to sustain the improvement after I left.

Diary Entry - The Leaf Insect

Towards the end of my second trip to the jungle I was still making observations in my diary. The following entry appears :

"On the rig in the jungle I am continually amazed at the number and diversity of the creatures that I find lying stunned in the compound in the morning. Some of them must be physically stunned from the impact with large pieces of oil rig equipment but there must be others who are completely sensible and are lying on the ground trying to work out what the hell it was they hit. "I've been flying around here minding my own business for years and I don't remember a big grey box ever being there before."

These poor creatures have evolved over the millennia to suit their particular niche in the environmental balance, and then we stick large grey objects in their path.

It is a bit more than a challenge to expect nature to adapt quite so quickly.

There is one creature I spotted that seemed particularly well suited though. It was about six centimetres long and only had four legs, it looked as if it wanted to be a large locust but being a bit short in the leg department settled for looking remarkably like a large green leaf, although I have to admit it looked suspiciously three dimensional to really get away with it on a clear day.

This creature was clearly depending to a large extent on the myopia of the rest of the jungle population for its own survival. The fact that I spotted it on the bonnet of a large white Ford Explorer suggested that it had one or two problems of its own in the eyesight department."

Chapter 6

Vente Cuatro

As the project on the rig progressed there began to be signs that something else was happening. The crews were beginning to enjoy their work. After three weeks the crew had skidded in under an hour and I had enjoyed collecting my beer. The crew had enjoyed skidding the rig faster than it had ever been done before, nobody had raised a voice, nobody ran and nobody felt any pressure. They were learning what it was like to be proud of themselves.

Werner, the Toolpusher, was enjoying the skids too. When everything was ready he would make a great show of taking his chair from his office out onto the concrete apron. He would sit with a cup of coffee doing absolutely nothing while in front of him the skid was carried out by a team of inexperienced, semi literate jungle Indians, better than he had ever seen it done in his life.

This was the first solid success and there was now an expectation that the crew would all sit down after the skid and collect the positives and negatives from each operation. I would simply take the notes and give the crew their amended checklist at the end.

It was time to turn my attention to something else.

I used to go up to the rig floor at odd times every day to talk to the members of each crew without any agenda. They would come and chat and I would ask them to explain some aspect of the operation or I would just spend time staring out over the jungle or watching a spectacular sunset. I had become part of the furniture and whatever operation was happening just continued around me.

The crews had settled into their stride with the skidding operation and now that Werner was also comfortable it was time to apply the process to other aspects of the drilling operations.

I would spend time watching the crew running the casing. The casing is run into the well after the drilling is complete to stop the hole from collapsing. These wells were drilled for about eighteen hundred metres then the casing was run into the hole in nine metre lengths. These lengths are called joints and would be taken up to the rig floor one at a time then screwed together and run into the hole.

The casing crew, when they had a minute, would chat or just lean on the rail and watch the jungle while they waited for the next joint to be made ready.

One evening while running casing everything was calm and peaceful and the only raised voice was when the driller was ready to make up the next joint. He would have to drag the crew's attention back from the jungle to the job in hand. I felt that I was setting a bad example by staring out at the jungle myself so I told the driller I was leaving.

I went down to the logging shack where all the times are recorded automatically and checked the casing running times. They were nearing the end of a run of casing and the average for the whole run was sixteen joints per hour. Curiously enough the count for the hour that I had been on the floor was twenty joints.

I was not altogether surprised. I had long been aware of the value of letting people know how they were doing. When people know that someone is paying attention to what they are doing their performance will invariably improve, for that reason alone.

Imagine the scenario. You are starting work on a production line and the supervisor tells you that your daily target is ten widgets per day. You look at the job and see that it is achievable so off you go. One day you forget the count and you realise that you have actually made eleven widgets. Whoops, but not to worry because at least you erred on the right side, and the supervisor can hardly shout at you for exceeding your quota.

But the supervisor doesn't notice, there is no summons to explain what happened so you go back to work. You say to yourself, "If no one cares then I am sure I will not produce eleven widgets again."

Life carries on until the day that you miscount again. This time you only produce nine widgets. Now you are in trouble.

But again, nobody notices. You wait for the reprimand for a whole week but nothing happens. Now you know that nobody gives a damn so nine becomes the norm. Then it slips to eight and again you wait for the inevitable reprimand, which doesn't come, "If they don't give a damn why should I?" Before you know it your average production is six, your machine is filthy and when someone finally suggests that you are not meeting your target you fire back with a tirade about the working conditions, the equipment, the stock and the impossibility of achieving a target that has been arbitrarily set by management.

Does that sound familiar?

Imagine the difference if when you accidentally made eleven widgets somebody had been paying attention and said thank you.

I produced graphs of the crew's performances, running casing, skidding, drilling, cementing, and posted them on the front gate. Everybody going in or out saw their performance and the crew knew that. The extra four joints that were run during the hour while I was on the floor were a result of someone paying attention.

It was logical after running the casing to bring the subject up at the next Charla. I asked the crew the same questions. What changes could they make to improve the job and what could they stop doing that was hindering them?

I talked to all four crews, asking them and facilitating the discussions to try to figure out what could be done to improve the performance. By the time I had finished the cycle of discussions with the crews it was only two days away from the next casing run and the list of ideas I had was a big fat zero. The crews had all the equipment they needed, everything worked the way it was supposed to, they had the casing and the manpower. What else could they do?

The rig was prepared and the casing run started.

That afternoon I was in the box I called my office when Cruz, one of the roustabouts, came running and put his head through the door. By this time there was a light and a door but the door was always propped open with the rock to keep the temperature bearable, the air conditioning was still uncontrollable.

Cruz was out of breath and excited and it was difficult for me to understand what he was saying at first. I finally realised that he wanted me to come and watch the casing run. Cruz was beside himself and almost dragged me outside and across the compound. The first thing I noticed was that everybody was smiling and giving the thumbs up. Cruz kept touching my watch and asking for the time. I realised that Cruz was asking me to time the operation so he could tell the crew how fast they were running the casing.

I pointed at the logging shack and explained that as the time was taken automatically in there, all that Cruz had to do was to ask.

He was off in a second and I headed up to the rig floor. As I came up the stairs I could see the same smiles all around. Everybody could sense that they were working well and Cruz had been despatched to get me to find out just how well they were doing.

When I got to the rig floor I was curious to find out for myself what the difference was between this run and the last one that I had observed.

The first thing I noticed was that nobody was looking at the jungle. Everyone was watching what was going on and was waiting to play his part. The driller said nothing. As soon as the casing was in position the crew were ready with the slips and tongs and when a new joint was required it was already at the rig floor waiting for the elevators to swing it into position. There was no waiting for anything. The crew still came over to talk to me but now instead of leaning on the rail looking outwards they would talk to me without their eyes leaving the rig floor where the casing was being run. Before they were needed they were back in position waiting to go. The smiles and the manic behaviour of Cruz made me think that they were on a high and perhaps working too fast. My first thought was that this could be when someone might get hurt. The more I watched the more I could see that the difference was that now the whole crew was working towards a common goal. Nobody had to ask or tell anyone what to do because the job was running on automatic, everyone knew what he had to do and was doing it without rushing. The men were impressed with themselves and they wanted to make sure that someone else was too.

Cruz came out of the logging shack with a huge smile and shouted so that everybody could hear, " Vente Cinco! Vente Cinco!"

There were high fives all round and then the crew settled back into the rhythm of the work. I left the floor and went back to the office to change the scale on my graph, I was going to need more room if they were going to continue running casing like this.

A short while later I had a visit from Luis the mud logger. Luis came from Merida, a beautiful old city in the mountains in the West of Venezuela. He was the man who ran the recording apparatus in the logging shack. He told me about Cruz coming in and asking to be shown how to read the charts so that he could tell the crew how fast they were running casing. I asked him if that had caused a problem. Cruz said no it hadn't, but it had never happened before and he was not sure if he should have given that information to a roustabout whose job was picking up pipe and delivering it to the rig floor.

Explaining to him why being able to see how they were doing meant everything to the crew. I asked him to recall how the crew looked and worked when they were running at sixteen joints per hour and what the difference was now that they were running at twenty five joints per hour. He looked thoughtful, so I asked him how he thought the crew felt just now, what could he see in their faces.

Luis said, "Now they are proud, they are proud to be running casing so fast." He became thoughtful again for a moment then he smiled and said, "Señor Peter, how could they be proud if they don't know how they are doing? I think I understand."

Luis sat with me for another twenty minutes over a cup of coffee and talked about Merida.

In the evenings it was my custom to take a walk around the compound before I went to bed. That night the crew were still running casing so I did not go up to the rig floor for fear of spoiling their new concentration. As I walked past the rig, the door to the logging shack was flung open and the night logger, Luis's relief, put his hand out and stuck a piece of paper to the outside of the shack. On it was written in large letters the number twenty four. He gave me a big thumbs up then ducked back in.

I looked up at the rig floor some nine metres above and could hear the number, "Vente Cuatro," being called up the derrick to the derrick-man and the roughnecks.

For that whole run the average was twenty four joints per hour. There were occasions when the rate went up to twenty five joints per hour but the average never exceeded twenty four.

When I met Duncan, the country manager, later that month I apologised that the rig had not been able to make the magical average of twenty-five joints per hour. Duncan did not look too worried, as he was still having a hard time believing that the crew had beaten twenty.

Casing was run in eight more wells before I left the rig. In seven out of the eight the average speed for running casing was twenty four joints per hour. On the occasion when they did not make twenty four there was a mechanical breakdown and the average was twenty two joints per hour. This was still two more than the target set by the country manager in Caracas that the crews had not been expected to achieve.

In most situations, the rig skidding being an example, the performance improvement comes from a combination of changes.

The most obvious and easily measured change comes from the way that the operation is physically carried out, i.e. the use of new tools or changes in the way in which old tools are used.

The less obvious change comes from a difference in the attitude of the people doing the job.

People generally want to do a good job. If they can see how they are doing they can take pride in their performance. When they have no way of knowing if they are doing a good job or not they lose interest and their performance becomes ordinary. On the rig I had allowed the crew to see how they were doing. During the casing running there were no changes in the equipment and no changes in procedure.

The crew were doing exactly the same job with exactly the same equipment but their performance went from sixteen joints per hour to twenty four joints per hour, a sustained fifty percent improvement.

By allowing the crews to see how they were performing they began to care about what they were doing and take pride. I had created the conditions which allowed the crews to take ownership and the crews had responded.

That was the difference.

Diary Entry - The Beetle

I was sitting in my office one afternoon writing up the crews' ideas for improvements when I was distracted by a beetle which seemed to be spending an inordinate time on its back on the desk. My diary reads :

"There is a peculiar kind of beetle in Venezuela that reminds me of a character in a book or perhaps a cartoon. It is a normal sized beetle with a little spike like a thorn on its back. It is an unremarkable brown colour and it flies around quite slowly in an aimless sort of fashion until it bumps into something. Unlike a fly it never seems to bump into windows, it is always something solid like a wall or a door.

It hits whatever it flies into then falls down onto the floor where it invariably lands on its back. There ensues a titanic struggle to get back onto its feet. As soon as it is the right way up it flies off in whichever direction it is facing. If that direction happens to be the wall too bad, it flies into it again and repeats the whole process. If it is facing in another direction it flies off happily until it makes contact with the next solid object. You have to ask yourself if, just before it hits the next solid object, a little thought doesn't flash across its mind, "Haven't I done this before?"

Chapter 7
Ownership

Ownership is a term that finds itself on the lips of managers too often and for the wrong reasons.

The function of a manager should be to support and find ways to encourage ownership in his staff, instead of using the lack of it as a vehicle to apportion blame.

Ownership is something which the workforce wants and it is usually discouraged by the things that the manager does.

On my rig in Venezuela there is a tool in the derrick called the grabber. This is a hydraulic clamp which is used to hold onto the top of the drill pipe to screw it into the previous section, this allows the hole to be drilled deeper. While drilling a deviated well, that is drilling at an angle (very few wells are drilled vertically these days) the joints of the drill pipe lie on the low side of the hole and when they are rotated the joints are eroded where they are in contact with the formation. To reduce this erosion the joints are protected by a band of very hard metal which is just proud of the softer steel of the drill pipe and therefore protects the joint.

When the grabber is used to make up a new joint the face of the clamp is dressed with very hard metal dies whose purpose is to bite into the softer steel of the drill pipe to give the grip which allows the pipe to be spun.

If the grabber is not positioned correctly the hard dies come into contact with the hard band on the pipe and there is no give. The first result is that there is no grip, the driller tries to spin the pipe but it will not spin and he has to stop. He has to relocate the jaws of the grabber onto the softer steel and try again.

The second and infinitely worse consequence of the grabber clamping on the hard banding is that the dies become stressed in a way for which they were never designed. When that happens they break and fall to the drill floor where the roughnecks are working. Each die weighs half a kilo which, landing on a roughneck after falling eighteen metres, will cause some damage.

In addition to the safety aspect, every time a die breaks the crew have to stop drilling for half an hour while it is replaced. I knew that they were suffering some downtime as a result of these dies breaking and having to be replaced but was assured that the situation was under control. After two months of the dies regularly breaking, without injuring anyone, I noticed that once again drilling had stopped and the grabber was being lowered again to change out more dies.

I was standing outside the office watching when Werner the Toolpusher saw me. He was on his way back to his office with a face like thunder and I could see that all was not well. Werner motioned me back inside the office and while I poured two cups of coffee and waited, he continued to fume.

"I am sick of telling these people what to do. I have been telling them for the last two months how to use that ******* grabber and here we are again, another hour lost and we are running out of dies. What the **** can we do?" For a German, Werner had a very good command of the use of stars in the English language.

I knew that Werner understood what was happening on the rig but under pressure, he had forgotten what he should be doing.

I asked him to go back over what he had just said and try to find out what it was he had been doing wrong. Werner had not really said much so it did not take him long to find the word in question. Almost immediately he said, "OK I get it, I have been "telling" them what to do, I know I should not be doing that but I have honestly had them up to here. Can you handle this for me?"

I said I would give it some thought. I asked Werner about his new daughter and we spent the rest of the time looking at baby pictures.

Most people enjoy telling other people what to do. There is a curious satisfaction called power which makes us feel good when we tell other people what to do. When we are in a position of authority we can achieve that feeling as many times as we want because people will always say yes, then go away and appear to do what they have been told. It makes us feel good.

Unfortunately telling other people what to do is probably the least effective way of achieving your goal. In some cases even less effective than doing it yourself, and that defeats the object of being a manager.

After we have learned how to perform a task we no longer need to be told what to do. If then we continue to be told what to do it feels insulting that your boss thinks so little of you he has to treat you as if you are an idiot.

How many times have we heard the complaint, "He's always telling me what to do".

If we feel upset or insulted then it is very unlikely that we will actually do what we have been told. Instead there are a number of options available to us :

1. We do nothing then report back to the manager that we have done what we were told to do. This makes the manager happy and gets him off our back.

2. We do what we were told but we do it slowly and badly, which makes us feel better.

3. We break what we were told to do. We feel even better about this course of action because we can shift the blame onto the manager. It was his fault for telling us to do it, and we then have the extra satisfaction of seeing how angry he becomes.

It sounds devious and nasty but unfortunately this is the way that human beings react to situations they don't like.

If you are reading this there is a good chance that you are a human being and you will recognise this behaviour in yourself at work and at home. We all have bosses in both places.

Werner recognised that he was doing the wrong thing but he also recognised that he was too close to the problem.

I thought about it for a while and the following day asked Werner if the crew had a written procedure for the use of the grabber. He told me there was one but the crew did not actually have a copy. "They shouldn't need one because they all know how to use the ******* thing."

I let that go. I asked Werner if it was OK to use the Charlas to help the crew write their own procedure for the operation of the grabber. He agreed.

I began at the next Charla by asking the crew what they thought important about the operation of the grabber.

What had they to do to make sure it operated correctly and what they had to avoid doing?

I asked each crew in turn and gradually built up a list of dos and don'ts that took shape as their own procedure. The final step was to get each crew to vet the final document and confirm that I had not left anything out.

I showed the final document to Werner. He read it and said, "I told you they knew how to use the grabber, this covers exactly the same points as our procedure which I have been trying to get them to understand all along."

I asked him if he could tell what the difference was between the two procedures. Werner rolled his eyes and said, "Yes," as if it was his five times table which he was being asked to recite for the umpteenth time.

He held out the two documents. "This is my procedure and this one belongs to the crew, they own it."

Werner knew the words but was yet to be convinced.

The following month I recorded as usual all the instances of non-productive time. There were no more instances of the dies in the grabber breaking. When I left the rig two months later they were still using the same set of dies. There had been no more breakages.

The week before I was due to leave the rig I was on my way up to the rig floor when I heard raised voices. As my head drew level with the floor I saw what was going on. The driller had positioned the grabber to spin up the pipe but before he clamped the pipe one of the roughnecks looked up and had seen that the grabber was going to bite the hard banding. He shouted at the driller to stop and look up.

The driller did so and looking sheepish apologised to the roughneck for forgetting. He changed the position of the jaws then re-clamped the pipe. It was not the roughneck's job to check the position of the grabber but when you own something you can't be selective about what you pay attention to.

When you care, you care about everything.

Werner had listened to what I was saying and understood intellectually the lesson that telling people what to do was wrong. For Werner however, all of his working experience had been filled with either being told what to do or telling other people what to do. That represented a powerful lot of negative conditioning that Werner had to overcome before his intellectual understanding became a belief that he could use to change his behaviour towards the crews.

By the time I left the rig Werner, having seen the practical results, had found his belief and was practising hard at his new skill of managing without telling people what to do.

He acknowledged to me that it was not an easy thing. He would have to physically stop himself when he found that he was about to issue an order. He would think about what it was he wanted to achieve before asking the questions which would allow the crew themselves to suggest the best way of achieving it. A big part of what Werner wanted to achieve was the continued development of the crews' sense of responsibility and ownership. Werner understood now how easy it was to damage their new sense of ownership by issuing orders that robbed them of the need to think.

He was beginning to understand what he could do to allow his people to become powerful.

Werner was doing very well.

Chapter 8

A Moving Story

There was one operation on the rig that I had never seen. That was the rig move. When all the wells on one site have been drilled the whole rig, the generators, the accommodation, the third party service companies, everything was packed up and moved bodily through the jungle to the next location where the whole drilling cycle would start again.

I had been on leave when the rig was moved and when I came back the crews were reassembling everything to recommence drilling. I checked the log and saw that the move which had been budgeted for two days, had actually taken five.

The drilling contractor had flown in their rig move specialist, Eric Hoffman. He came from Germany for the event. His full time job was moving rigs. When he arrived he naturally took charge, and was still on site so I spoke to him about the operation and how he thought it had gone.

Eric said he was quite pleased. It had been difficult and he had not had much sleep but he thought that everybody had worked hard and with the exception of a few mechanical breakdowns the operation had progressed well.

When I asked him about the time it had taken, he did not seem too concerned that it had taken three days more than planned. Eric said that the rig manager always set impossible times, so it took as long as it took. I left Eric with Werner and went to put the times for the move up on the gate where all of the performance graphs were displayed for the crew to see. I waited while the next crew bus arrived. They came off the bus and went straight to the new graph where they started an animated discussion amongst themselves. I gave them a few minutes to get changed then went to meet them at the Charla.

Normally there was a good deal of banter and joking at these meetings but today there was an atmosphere. I asked them to tell me what they were concerned about. The floodgates opened and they all started shouting at once how it was unfair to measure the time of the rig move because it wasn't their fault.

They told me how Eric had arrived two days before the move and had not talked to anyone about what he proposed to do or how he proposed to do it. When the day to move arrived he came on site and just started telling everyone what to do. The sub contractor brought in to handle the move had turned up with the wrong trucks and when one of them broke down they could not do anything for half a day until a new one arrived because each load had to be moved in the correct order. When one load could not be moved due to a breakdown it held up the whole operation. If Eric was not physically on site, when he was eating or sleeping, the whole operation ground to a halt because if he was not personally directing nobody else could. He was the only person who knew the plan because it was all in his head.

The meeting was rapidly degenerating into a shouting match as all of their frustrations came out. I allowed it to go on for a few minutes and then the driller stood up to quieten the crew down. As the last of the shouting died away I asked the driller what was the one detail which would have made the move better for them.

He looked around the crew for a few moments in silence then said, "We should have been told the plan."

Having talked to Eric, I knew that there was no plan other than what was in Eric's head, so I asked the crew where they thought they could get this plan from.

The driller looked around at the faces of the crew then said, "We could make one" and looking around the crew I could see from their faces that this was something that they were all happy with. After that, at every Charla for the next three weeks there was only one topic of conversation and that was "The Plan."

Each crew took up from where the last one left off and they started to dissect the operation.

A Moving Story

First was the order that the equipment had to be moved. What had to be left to last and what could be moved before drilling stopped. How many loads there were, how many people were needed to prepare, load and unload each one. Then how many trucks were needed and when did they need them, what happened if they lost a truck.

Slowly the crew built the plan up until every piece of equipment had been accounted for and could be traced through the plan from decommissioning on one site through to re-commissioning on the new site, when it was going to happen, who was going to do it and what equipment was required to make it happen.

The crews created their plan on the board in their shack and every shift I would transfer the new plan to the computer and brief Werner on the progress they were making.

Werner recognised immediately the power of what was happening. He'd had his lesson and now he could see the crews getting involved in an operation which in normal circumstances he himself would leave to the expert who was flown in for the purpose.

The project was now maturing and I was able to leave more and more to the crews. They were enjoying being in control and Werner was enjoying the freedom it gave him to run the rig instead of standing over them in every little task.

This is the time when my work was done. The change was apparent and the crew were in charge of their own rig.

Werner understood how the change had occurred and what he had to do to support it.

The time was close for me to leave.

As I packed for the last time I got a call from Willie. I always stopped to see him on the way out of the country but this time he asked me if he could bring the crews' plan for the rig move.

I had asked Werner to start attending the Charlas and for the last few days I stopped going while he finished off the plan with the crews.

I met Willie in El Tigre and with him were the contractors who were due to supply the trucks and moving equipment for the next rig move.

The contractors were a worried bunch, as the last move had taken so long, some of the delays definitely being their fault, that Willie had withheld part of their payment. Their long faces suggested that they were expecting more bad news.

Without any preamble Willie introduced me and told the contractors that I was going to tell them how to move the rig next time.

I looked up at Willie as he said this and saw that he realised what he had done. He looked sheepish. It was taking some getting used to, to understand how unproductive "telling" people what to do really was. At least Willie understood and was trying.

With my happy face on I introduced myself to the three contractors in turn then suggested that we all had a coffee before we made a start.

This broke the ice and a few minutes later we sat down to start again. I asked the contractor what they thought they could do differently next time to try to get a better result for the rig move. They went quiet for a moment then the boss, Enrique, said that he didn't see what he could do differently, he just supplied the trucks he was told to supply and did what he was told by the rig-move specialist, Eric.

I asked if he would like to take a look at an idea which the crews had been working on that might make a difference.

Unfolding the printout of the crews' plan I started to run through it with the contractors. In no time at all they took over the floor, and were talking so fast and excitedly that I lost the thread of their Spanish and could barely understand what they were saying. The contractors had caught on immediately to the value of the plan and were out of their seats crowding around the table to get a better look.

Sitting back, I let them get on with it. I looked across at Willie and caught the ghost of a wink through his smile.

My attention was dragged back to the table, where it's contractors were asking about a spare line in the plan which did not seem to connect with anything else. I explained that this was the spare truck, the crews' idea.

The truck had its own work to do but none of the loads were dependent on anything else. If another truck broke down then this truck could be taken immediately from its task to take over until another truck came from their base. Any disruption would be minimal and when the new truck arrived the spare could go back to its allotted tasks.

Having been penalised for lost time due to mechanical breakdowns during the last move the contractors could appreciate that this was a clear and valuable change to the operation.

I lost track of their conversation again and suddenly they were all leaving. Willie told me that they were going to fetch their boss.

Fifteen minutes later they were back with the roundest man I have ever seen. It was clear why he didn't get out much. He was assisted into a chair and prepared himself to be convinced.

I motioned to Enriques to speak and the party started again. Two hours later Willie and Enriques had agreed all of the logistical details and the contract was passed to Señora Santa, Willie's secretary, for typing.

There was one more stop to make. I had a few hours before my flight from El Tigre and Willie asked if I would mind accompanying him to the offices of the field manager. These were the offices in which four months earlier Willie had been told in no uncertain terms that if the performance of the rig did not improve they could pack up and take it back to Europe. Willie was clearly looking forward to this visit.

Pablo Lopez was the field manager, who in my four months in the field I had never met.

Willie introduced me as the consultant who had been helping them on the rig and left it at that. Pablo was clearly still thinking of his last conversation when he had threatened to remove Willie and was giving all the signals of a man who was too busy to be bothered with excuses and had to move on to more important things.

I said nothing and waited for him to open the conversation. If he was so busy he would have to say something just to get rid of us.

Finally Pablo asked what it was that I did, in a tone that said, "I don't really care, I just want to get this conversation over and you out of my office."

I told him that I did absolutely nothing, and waited for Pablo to speak again.

After an elongated pause Pablo said, "You must have done something, you have been on the rig for the last four months." Now he was actually asking so I told him that the people who had actually "Done something" were the crew. Did he want to see what it was that the crew had done?

This time Pablo gave up and smiled, he knew when he had been beaten. "Yes," he said, "Show me what the crews have done." He put his pen down then sat back with folded arms to listen.

I had graphics with me which had been prepared for Willie as part of the end of project package but, as there was no projector and no slides, I referred to the printout of the project report.

It was a simple story about the crew astonishing everybody with the speed that they skidded the rig, how they wrote their own procedures to use the grabber and the difference that made, how they ran casing as fast as it had ever been run in the world and how they did it time after time. It was about the crews taking control of moving the rig from site to site. It was about creating the conditions for ownership and what happened when the crews took it.

A Moving Story

The presentation lasted less than twenty minutes, simply outlining what had happened and why.

At the end of it the first question Pablo asked was how long I could stay for. I had intended spending some more time with Willie before getting on the plane but looking at Willie I could tell that this was where he wanted me to spend that time. I told Pablo that if we went straight to the airport I could stay for another two hours, maximum.

Pablo asked if I was prepared to give the presentation again and whether he could make the graphics into slides. He disappeared and coffee was brought in, then a projector, and finally a girl arrived and took the project report away to produce the slides.

Pablo came back after twenty minutes, almost as if he was checking that Willie and I were still there. After another twenty minutes he ushered in two Americans. I recognised them as the rig managers, essentially doing Willie's job, for two competing drilling contractors in the same field.

Pablo sat down, introduced them and asked me to start again.

This time I was using the slides and the show went well. At the end I could see some concern on the two newcomers' faces." Where is this going? What has this got to do with us?"

I had an idea where it was going, I sat down and left the floor to Pablo. He pulled no punches and, predictably, told them that if they did not start to do with their rigs what Willie had done with his they could pack up and go home to the United States.

I left Venezuela for the last time that evening. I was happy that in Willie and Werner I had left people who understood when to let go and have faith in the ability of others, people who understood and had seen first hand the futility of trying to maintain control by telling people what to do. They had seen the difference and I felt sure that their crews were in good hands. Pablo told the two other contractors that they should hire me, but they didn't. Why should they?

81

If Pablo had asked them how they thought they could improve then perhaps they would have suggested hiring me for themselves. Instead Pablo was telling them what to do and they easily found reasons why they should not. We have already seen the way that humans react when they are told what to do and the contractors' reaction was perfectly normal.

I phoned Werner later that month from a new project I was starting in the North Sea. He told me that when Eric had arrived to move the rig he had once again slipped into the role of controller and started to run the rig move to his own secret agenda. The crews through the drillers had demanded a meeting and had explained their plan to Eric.

Eric was amazed, in all his experience he had never seen a plan to move a rig before and he agreed that the crews had a much better way. Now at the beginning of each eight-hour shift Eric would sit down with the whole crew at the Charla to discuss progress so far and the plan for the next eight hours.

The rig move was accomplished in two and a half days, including the time it took to replace two of the trucks that broke down.

I was happy. The crew were looking after themselves and the managers were supporting the crews. They had got it right.

There are plenty of people left like Pablo and the other rig managers. Most of us are those people. It takes a little thought and a lot of faith to make the first step from "Telling" people what to do to "Asking" what they think would work best. Once that step is made and the amazing power of people becomes apparent, it is a very easy change to accept.

Chapter 9

Marche

Marche (Pronounced "Marsh"), on the trail in Northern Canada this was the word which was translated as "Mush" and was used to drive the dog teams which were once the only source of power in the frozen North.

What was not translated was the original meaning of the word "Marche" which was the French imperative "Walk".

Not run, not hurry up or go faster, just walk.

There are in fact only three orders which the dog team understand, "Stop", "Go", and "Take it easy".

In the company of several business colleagues, I was lucky enough to take a dog sledding tour in Canada with "Snowy Owl Tours" under the careful tutelage of Connie Arsenault.

Connie's father was a park ranger in Alberta. She grew up in the wilderness in the company of independent natives, and an odd selection of geologists and naturalists.

She first developed her interest in dogs' speed racing over shorter distances, then she graduated to the longer distance Iditerod and Yukon Quest events. Connie is also the co-founder of the Alberta International Sled Dog Classic and runs Snowy Owl Sled Dog Tours with her husband Charles.

She said, "Dogs are so much like people that in fact I have learned more about people working with my dogs than anything I have done with people. There are some surprising differences though. Dogs are the most forgiving creatures I know, people are not!"

She began the tour by introducing our group to the dogs with an attention to detail born of a genuine respect and care for her teams, and explained how the teams worked.

All the dogs are attached to the sledge by one common line to which each individual is attached by a separate harness. The direction of this line is the direction the sledge will take and each animal's effort can be gauged by his alignment to the direction of travel of the sledge.

Connie talked about the importance of selecting the correct dogs for each team. Their position in the team being determined by their size, level of courage and willingness to perform. She explained how it all worked.

"When we are laying our dogs out in a team we have front to rear, lead dogs, point dogs, swing dogs and wheel dogs."

In an eight dog team of four pairs the first pair are the lead dogs. They are not the strongest but they have the intelligence, focus, character and speed which allow the other dogs to follow. If the lead dog does not lead, the team will not follow and the sledge will go nowhere.

Next are the point dogs, who are the apprentice lead dogs and are usually yearlings.

At the back of the team are the wheel dogs. These two are the powerhouse of the team, strong and undramatic, they take their direction, then putting their shoulders to the traces, they get the job done.

In the middle is the schoolyard, with the swing dogs. This pair will usually consist of a young dog and an older dog, perhaps an old lead dog or a wheel dog who is getting on in years and has been replaced in his principal position by a younger more capable dog.

His usefulness is not over, strength is not the only commodity valued in this team. The old dog in the schoolyard, or swing position now has the job of bringing on the younger dog through his example and experience. He in turn responds to and gains fresh energy from the enthusiasm of the younger dog.

These eight dogs will comfortably haul three people all day, or they will equally happily fight and play in the snow. These eight individuals make up the team. The driving is done exclusively by praise and recognition. Praise for the team effort and for the individual.

Connie explained the significance of our position relative to the dog team. She said that we were a part of the team but like the dogs, we still had to earn the right to be there. Unless we were prepared to jump off the sledge and give the dogs a hand when they needed it, the dogs would lose respect and stop pulling. That included helping out by pushing when going uphill and holding the sledge back so it didn't overrun the dogs going down hill. Our job was not to tell the team what to do, they already knew that better than we did. Our job was to provide the physical and verbal support the dogs needed to tell them that their efforts were appreciated.

She explained, "There are no passengers on a sledge."

Connie's reason for making this statement was because she cared for her teams and did not want them to be annoyed or upset through accidental mishandling or abuse.

There was a worried question from one of my colleagues. "What happens if we get it wrong?" I could see the picture he had in his mind, him hanging on grimly while his baying team headed for the horizon at top speed, out of control. Connie saw it too and had the answer perfectly.

She told us, "If you are in charge of a team and you get it wrong the team will cease to function. That means they will stop pulling in the same direction and therefore be incapable of taking off towards any horizon. They will let you know long before that all is not well. All you have to do is watch for the signs that they will give you."

She said, "The first thing you have to understand is that these are working dogs. Dogs who get so excited at the prospect of pulling that at the beginning of the day when they are fresh they will often go too fast and need to be controlled by the use of the brake."

"If you stick to the three instructions they know and understand "Stop," "Go," "Take it easy," and give them the support that they need then they will do their best for you."

"If you confuse them with unnecessary or contradictory orders, or shout at them, they will stop working as a team."

"They will take their weight off the harness while still keeping it taut to make it look as if they are working, or they will simply wander off line and start eating snow or fighting."

She said that the first sign of this in the team is when the dogs start to look over their shoulders at the driver. Normally the lead dog is the first, he turns around while still pulling and in his eyes you can see what is in his mind. He is saying, "Just let me know what you want and I will do it". or "We are doing our best, why don't you get off and help instead of doing all that shouting?"

Unless you pay attention to these first signs, the breakdown of the team will follow.

Connie told a great story but we were impatient to board our sledges and set off up the trail behind our teams.

I was paired initially with a guide, who started the dogs and stopped them and told me when to jump on the brake. The whole of the rest of the time she spent praising the team and the individuals. At first I thought that she was making too much of this support and puzzled at the meticulous way she named and praised each of the dogs individually, encouraging them, then returning to give renewed praise for the whole team. Initially it seemed like overkill and I could see no effect.

What that really meant was, the team just did what I expected a dog team to do. They didn't make a fuss, they pulled together in the same direction and they kept their eyes to the front, except to occasionally acknowledge with a glance the guide's words of encouragement, as if the dogs knew that she also needed to know that her efforts were appreciated.

There was a lot of shouting and noise coming from the sledge behind.

They did not have a guide of their own and my guide, Katherine, had to keep stopping to allow them to catch up. Kath had her hands full trying to pour an equal amount of attention both on our team, and the team behind who were clearly not enjoying themselves at all and needed help.

It was then I realised that what she was doing was almost a physical thing. She was not just being nice to the dogs. She was providing the fuel that the teams needed to work. Without the support that she was providing for her team, the team behind was falling apart. The more the dogs ceased to function as a team the more their driver shouted and cajoled and directed. That was exactly the behaviour which Connie said would stop the team from functioning, and she was right.

At the halfway point some of the group changed sledges and I found myself with the team which had been behind for the journey out. One of the drivers from the outward leg also stayed with that team.

We set off again for the return with a chorus of shouts and whistles all intended by my new driver to motivate and push the team to greater effort. It was apparent that this confusing set of signals was not doing the job. The dogs were turning around and looking at the driver, they weren't pulling and the sledge was not moving.

More shouts were added and my driver launched into a litany of the faults of the team and how it really was spoiling his day that he had such an awful team.

I remembered Connie's words and thought we should try something different. I said to my driver, "Why don't we just save our breath and see what the dogs will do on their own?"

He stopped shouting and gave up his position to me.

With a spoken "Hike up" (The modern version of "Mush") the dogs pricked up their ears, faced the front and started pulling. I didn't give another order to the dogs. They knew where they were going. We helped going up the hills by scooting or running alongside and we braked going down. The rest of the time was spent providing the team with the fuel they needed to do their jobs. "Good job puppies, good puppies, well done Misty, good boy Laredo, well done Midnight, good girl Mexico, good boy Butch, well done Sundance, good girl Cinder, good dog Butte, good Boys! Good Girls!

And just once, I caught a kind of a backward glance from Laredo, who seemed to be saying, "See, now you've got it," and then he was back to his job of keeping up with the sledge in front and looking after the youngster at his shoulder.

The reason for explaining to us the dynamics of the team was not because Connie Arsenault had heard a theory about the principles of leadership and teamwork and was trying it for size.

The reason was that she raced dog teams the same way they have been raced for three hundred years. She knew that working with the team, not against them, was the only way to win.

Most people know intuitively how to make a team work. The team needs respect, support and space to perform in. If they do not have it they will cease to function as a team. As a group of individuals they do not have the direction or cohesive power to make anything happen at all.

Connie's story is true and is a reinforcement of what I knew to be true in my work with teams of people.

In the dogs I saw some basic truths about behaviour that humans have been aware of for centuries. I could see through the example of the dogs how the lessons applied to the modern team environment. The analogy works and gives a graphic insight into what makes a team work, and strikingly, what stops it from working.

Connie showed me two important lessons that day.

To make a significant change in our effectiveness we don't always have to do anything extra. All we have to do is to recognise what we are doing wrong, or what is not helping, then stop doing it. If shouting at the team is not working, stop doing it.

The other lesson that Connie showed me with the dog teams was the effect that the driver had on the team.

The driver (or manager) is responsible for performance but not in the way that we traditionally think. Telling the team what to do through unnecessary orders or shouting creates a very negative effect that is actually destructive.

What Connie showed us is that the driver creates the conditions under which the team works. It is those conditions which govern the performance of the team.

I had seen the difference in performance in one team under two different drivers. The only difference was the change in the conditions which the drivers had made for the team. The first driver had cursed and blamed the team but, the real fault lay with the person who created the conditions for failure, the driver.

Failure is not the fault of the team, it is the fault of the driver who creates the conditions which cause them to fail.

Understanding this distinction and how to create the right conditions which allow the team to perform is a key lesson for managers of the human team.

I was humbled to discover the clarity of the example that Connie and her dog teams had set for us.

Chapter 10

Cause And Effect

While working in the North Sea I heard a supervisor say of his team in frustration, "There is no point in treating them like adults when they behave like children."

I thought about the chicken and the egg, which came first? The team acting like children or someone treating them like children?

I was reminded very much of the story of the dog team in the last chapter. In the story, the dog team would not move and the driver was very vocal in his condemnation of them for their failure to pull. It wasn't until the driver started behaving differently that he realised the dog team was fine. It was his own behaviour which was making the dogs act the way they did.

The supervisor, who was called Rob, was in his early thirties and had not been in his position long. He had not grasped the idea that his behaviour was responsible for the behaviour of his team and did not see that it was the way in which he treated the crew which caused them to behave in the way they did. As far as he was concerned it was because they were a bad crew.

Rob had come up through the ranks and with a bit of attitude and application had found himself in the position of team leader. The nature of the industry meant that he was constantly in communication with his team and was accustomed to issuing rapid-fire instructions which had to be carried out instantly. Needless to say there was a fair amount of backchat but as team leader he was used to dealing with it and the banter helped the team through the day.

He was a good team leader and therefore the natural choice when the supervisor's job became vacant. He was young and flattered, he took the promotion.

When I met Rob he was not enjoying life at all. At work he was being subjected to personal attacks and abuse, both verbal and written. These attacks all emanated from the team over which his authority was expected to extend. Rob's reaction, like that of the dog team driver, was to become aggressive and heap the blame on the behaviour of his team with phrases like :

"There is no point treating them like adults
when they act like children."

It took a long time for Rob to understand the real point, if you treat people like adults they will behave like adults. If they are behaving like children, ninety-nine times out of a hundred it is because they are being treated like children.

The manager's behaviour influences the teams' behaviour. When a manager can influence behaviour then he has to accept responsibility for the behaviour he creates in others.

What a manager says and does has a direct effect on the behaviour of the members of his team, beyond the meaning of the words he is using.

We have all heard the expression "My door is always open," which is supposed to mean, "I am always approachable, you can always talk to me," but how often does the behaviour of the individual indicate exactly the opposite?

"My door may be open but you had better have a very good reason if you come through it."

Generally managers do believe that they influence their team's behaviour in the short term because managers like to feel that their team listen to and act on every word they say. (See on page 120 the discussion of the ABC Model for the effective alternative strategy to telling people what to do.)

Unfortunately there is a reluctance for the manager to accept responsibility for the longer-term consequences of his influence on the team.

What had started for Rob's team as another unremarkable supervisor had over time developed to the level where it was not uncommon for Rob and members of his team to be standing toe-to-toe shouting at one another.

Oddly enough it was my coaching using the analogy of the dog sledding story which provided the catalyst to let Rob see that he was the cause, and his team's behaviour was the effect.

Perhaps it was also the fact that Rob was so close to the end of his tether that he was able to ask of himself in all honesty whether he was the chicken or the egg. This is the way he explained it to me.

He said, "If you treat people like they are worth nothing, that is the way they will act. If you treat them as if they are valued then they will become valuable."

He had taken the biggest most significant step in acknowledging what it was to be a leader, that what he does influences the behaviour of others.

I realised that on the back of Rob's new understanding there was a great deal of coaching and support work to be done to allow him to fully utilise the power of his new knowledge. Unfortunately the project was concluding and I found myself being moved on.

My last meeting left Rob exploring ways to redress the balance.

There were a thousand things I could have suggested to help him to use his new understanding to change his behaviour. I didn't suggest any of them. I knew that having acknowledged that he was responsible for the behaviour of his team, Rob was the best person to decide what the changes were that he needed to make to start acquiring the behaviour he wanted from his team.

Chapter 11

Eddie

In the late nineties I was working as a performance coach in the northern North Sea on a drilling project which was fairly typical of the times.

My job was to implement the Breaking the Mould process with the drilling crew. The steps of this process were quite straightforward:

Begin each operation with a planning session. When the operation is complete hold a debriefing session.

When the operation is carried out again, everything learned from the last execution is incorporated into the new plan.

This has two effects. The first is that the team begin to achieve quantifiable performance improvements.

The second is that as a result of involving all levels of the team in the planning and debriefing process, the individual crew members become involved in decisions about what they do and they get an understanding of why they are doing it. This is the beginning of the road to ownership.

My job in the next year was to take them along the road to ownership until they could see where it was going and complete the journey for themselves.

The crew had been together for quite a number of years and with a few exceptions they were fairly close.

One of the exceptions was an assistant driller called Eddie. He was older than the average assistant driller but had found a level in the team which he enjoyed and he was happy to stay there.

Eddie was married with three children and was a part time farmer on The Isle of Skye. Before I arrived on the rig Eddie had started a correspondence with an English woman who bred border collies. He wanted to purchase a working dog for his croft. The woman however soon turned her attention to Eddie and started bombarding him when he was offshore with letters full of her burning passion. She had clearly never seen Eddie. He was six feet two bent double and after an afternoon of professional grooming on his wild mane of greying hair could have passed for a cross between someone auditioning for Jethro Tull and Catweazle. A fashion writer would have struggled to find a word between unkempt and wildman to apply to Eddie.

Nevertheless he was bombarded by the English dog breeder's letters and the evidence was, in the time honoured offshore tradition, displayed on the notice board for all to enjoy.

For those not familiar with the organisation of a drilling team there are a few things to understand about the way it works.

At the core of the team are the Roughnecks and Roustabouts. The Roughnecks work on the rig floor where the drilling is done and the Roustabouts work on the pipe deck delivering equipment to the rig floor.

In overall charge of the Roughnecks is the Driller, who has a sidekick called the Assistant Driller, then there is the Derrick Man and the Assistant Derrick man and next in line are the Roughnecks themselves. These are the men who physically drill the well. In overall charge of the team is the Toolpusher. The Toolpusher and his crew are all contractors so the drilling team has another two members who are the representatives of the Oil Company for whom the contractors are drilling the wells. They are called the Company Man and his assistant, the Drilling Engineer. The Company man is in overall charge of the whole drilling team. Operations tend to be twenty-four hours a day, seven days a week. There is one team working during the day and one at night. Each crew works a two week hitch offshore and then has a two week hitch at home while their opposite number is offshore on the rig.

I noticed that the closeness of these crews became more evident whenever their employers were mentioned. Their opinion about the company they worked for was unanimous and not very flattering.

Eddie

On this rig the Company Men and Drilling Engineers were not very happy either. They felt they were being asked to drill increasingly demanding wells with fewer resources.

The crews, discouraged by the lack of tangible success were being asked to commit more of their free time, onshore and off, to safety training or management initiatives. These generally consisted of turning up somewhere and staying awake while someone talked in an earnest way. While the speaker thought this tone of voice projected sincerity, it was actually received by the audience as, "Another load of rubbish that we have to sit through before they will give us our money for this month."

There was another reason that morale was not very high. Six months previously, the rig had been visited by a Management Consultant who had done a solid if unimaginative job. He turned up, wrote an exhaustive report then recommended that twenty percent of the crews be sacked. This was exactly the report which was required by the client. The changes were made so fast that heads spun.

Then I turned up. "Yes I am a Management Consultant" The answer to their first question went down like a lead balloon. It seemed that the wind was blowing in the wrong direction. Rather than waste energy fighting their preconception I turned and ran before it. I did not want to be in the defensive situation of having to explain why I was different to the other guys who also called themselves Management Consultants.

I was reminded of the story of the man who walked into a bar. When he had everybody's attention he said that he would just like everybody to know that he was not a rapist, "No sir, I am definitely not a rapist. Just wanted to make sure you all understood that."

Two minutes later one of the regulars said to his friend, "Where did that guy go?"

"Which one?" his friend replied.

"The rapist"

Instead of being shot for being a "Management Consultant" I settled down to become "The Planning Guy".

Eddie, during the difficult early days of the project when I definitely was a rapist, was one of the few crew members who always managed to stop for a gossip or to relay the latest chapter in his extraordinary love life, in case I had not had read it on the notice board.

The deck I was playing with had been heavily stacked against me by the crews' recent experience with consultants and progress was initially slow. The rig went through a succession of Company Men on one hitch who had me continually going back to square one to restart their coaching and on the other hitch was a man who was "The Boss". If anyone interfered, expressed an opinion or disagreed then Mike, who was that man, was a management scythe who felled all before him. He was vastly experienced at the business of drilling and guarded that experience jealously. He would not allow anyone else's opinion to obscure the fact that he was in charge.

Very early in the project Mike realised that planning meetings and debriefs were being designed to allow other peoples' opinions to be heard. His reaction was to ban them from his office. He refused to attend and barred his Drilling Engineer from attending either. In this situation I had the senior man and his assistant refusing to take part in any planning meetings and withdrawing the use of the room which had been designed to hold them in. This situation, described at the time as 'a little difficult,' was actually key to the success of the project.

The situation I found myself in provided the opportunity to make a fresh start and I invested my time coaching the individual crew members on how to run their own meetings.

I had found that in a planning meeting the person who takes the chair is normally the most senior person present. He is after all normally 'The Boss'.

But the fact that he is the boss and therefore probably has the widest practical experience of the operation, is precisely why he is the worst person to chair the meeting.

If the chairman is greatly experienced in the practicalities of the execution of the task under consideration he should be giving one hundred percent of his attention to the subject in hand. He should not be distracted by trying to run the meeting as well.

What usually happened with Mike's meetings, was that he would take the chairman's role and use that position to tell everybody what to do, which made him feel wise and powerful.

Unfortunately behaviour like that makes everybody else feel patronised and demeaned. The crews also became angry because they were not being asked for, or given, the opportunity to voice their own opinions.

It is even harder with a strong boss to disagree or make suggestions. The less forward members of the crew who rarely say anything feel patronised by the whole affair, they know they will never be asked to contribute and cannot see any purpose in being in the meeting other than to act as a captive audience for the chairman while he pontificates.

With me the crew all took turns at being chairman. Initially most were very wary of putting their heads on the block but all, with the exception of one, after a fifteen minute coaching session just before the meeting, came out of the meeting smiling. The exception was again Eddie. He flatly refused to have anything to do with the chairman's position saying, "It's not my job, why should I? He (Mike) should be doing it."

The reason that the crews were initially nervous of taking over as chairman was that the only experience they had of meetings was being on the receiving end of their boss's diatribes. If they were ever invited to a planning meeting then they knew two things. First, their boss would waffle on forever and second, they would never be asked for their opinion.

Not a very positive experience.

Now I was asking them to become the chairman and the cause of their unease was that firstly, they feared that they did not have enough experience to drone on for the same length of time as their boss, even allowing for the number of times that he would normally digress and repeat himself. Secondly, they knew that after a planning meeting they always resented the chairman for wasting their time and telling them information which they either already knew or they had no interest in. Now they were the ones who were going to be resented. They found the prospect of turning into their own worst enemy very unsettling. To their credit, in every case but one, Eddie, they were willing to give it a go.

The fifteen minute coaching session before their experience as chairman concentrated on one thing only, to ensure that they had a positive experience.

I made and plasticised small prompt sheets called 'The Chairman's Card' and the coaching session took the new chairman through these simple rules.

The Chairman's Card

1. The chairman has a job to do in a meeting. That job is to allow other people to speak and gather their ideas.

2. The chairman should not offer his opinion on anything. He should ask others for their opinion.

3. Nobody should leave the meeting without having been given the opportunity to express their opinion or give the meeting the benefit of their experience.

The Meeting

1. Before the meeting read the agenda.

2. Introduce the subject of the meeting and ask someone else to talk the meeting through the plan.

3. When actions are identified ensure someone is nominated to carry them out.

4. Ask each person to discuss their nominated Action Points to confirm clarity and agreement.

5. Ask if there is anything else that can be done to prepare before the operation commences.

6. Ask if there is any other equipment or method we could use to help us perform this job better.

7. Make sure that everybody present has spoken.

8. Don't allow the meeting to slowly dissolve into factions. When business is complete say "Thank you very much" and close the meeting.

The rules were designed to allow the chairman to concentrate on the dynamics of the meeting by taking no part in the actual discussion.

The reason the card was used was to allow the chairman during the meeting, if necessary, to read them and refocus himself on his job.

The last thing to do was to remind the new chairman that he was on his own. It was important that he knew he was going to conduct the meeting without help. I agreed with each chairman that if they used my name I would step in and help, but nobody ever did. It was difficult at times to avoid eye contact when I could feel someone was in trouble, but nobody ever gave up and they all agreed that the struggle to find their own way intensified the learning experience.

After the meeting, as with every operation, I held a short debriefing with the chairman.

It is the easiest thing in the world to stand in front of someone junior and tell him or her exactly what they are doing wrong. The criticism may even be correct but if it is given, what was a carefully orchestrated learning experience is destroyed by the act of telling someone what they did wrong. Not only is the experience itself compromised, any residual learning which may have been transferred through the debriefing will also be lost.

Going the other way is also not a good idea. In Europe if you praise someone who has not performed well he knows you are buttering him up and will just wait patiently for the criticism which he knows will come at the end. Normally it will be prefaced after a period of gushing praise by a phrase such as, "There is just one small thing I think I should mention".

If criticism is not made there is a loss of respect because the individual is aware that the coach is afraid to give it.

The dilemma; if we criticize we produce a negative experience and we lose the value of learning from a positive experience, and if we praise we run the risk of being vilified for being manipulative.

The answer I used? I asked the chairman how he thought he did.

That simple. The coaching session using 'The Chairman's Card' is fresh in the chairman's mind, he probably still has the card in his hand, so this is the best time to ask the question, "How do you think that went?"

I am continually amazed at the amount and accuracy of the criticism that people are willing to level at themselves but would never accept from anyone else. I never forgot to ask the chairman what he thought went well too.

The last question I always asked was, "What is the one thing that you are going to do differently next time?" It did not matter whether I agreed or not with what they said, we are all different. The point to understand is that if someone is clear about what he is trying to achieve he will get there in his own way. If the new chairman chooses a different path, as long as his objective is clear, to get the most value from the meeting, then I would support his choice of path. This maintains the positive aspect of the whole experience and respects the chairman's individuality.

When each crewmember had been chairman once, nearly four months later, I started to repeat the sequence. I repeated the coaching process, reminding each of them in turn of the rules and then I asked what they were going to concentrate on in this meeting. They all remembered the one thing they had said they were going to do differently from four months ago, and they all did it.

Two months later, six months after the ban on planning meetings Mike, the Company Man, asked if he could attend the next one. During that whole six months I had made sure that he knew what was happening, the progress that was being made, and why it was important.

This was a very difficult period for Mike. He was the 'boss' and one of the reasons that he was the boss was that he was a very strong and controlling character. It is not too difficult to imagine how much it would hurt someone like that to have a Management Consultant put on his team. It gives him a very strong message. "There is something wrong with the management (meaning you!) and this person is going to fix it."

The one thing that all bosses (the word is used deliberately, instead of manager) have in common is that they are not stupid. If they can see the value in something then unless the door has been slammed in their face they will want to use that value.

In the same way that the path each individual will take towards a common goal is different, it is also true that each individual's understanding is time dependent. Different people when presented with the same information will take a different length of time to reach their conclusion. I was only too aware that trying to achieve understanding any faster only creates resistance, which will only serve to slow down the process of change overall.

The harder someone tries to sell you a car the more reluctant you are to buy it because you want time to make up your own mind.

During the period of the meeting ban Mike, the Company man, was having a really hard time trying to figure out what was being done to him. His ego was dented badly and it took a long time for that to heal before he could apply himself intellectually to what was happening.

If at any time during those six months the door had been slammed on Mike, or if I had tried to hard-sell him on the process, his resistance to the changes would have grown to such a level that he may never have been able to see the benefit. By giving him the space and time he needed Mike was able to come to his own decision and when he rejoined the team he quickly became a champion of the Breaking the Mould process.

He didn't get away scot-free when he rejoined the meetings. The first meeting which he attended was being chaired by Danny, one of the roustabouts whose duties more normally consisted of directing the crane to move equipment around the pipe deck.

We had our preparation session as usual and Danny remembered the one thing he was not going to do, he was not going to get involved in the debate. This had happened on his first time round as chairman and immediately his control of the meeting had evaporated. Danny had struggled and eventually managed to regain control by force. Afterwards he said that he knew the instant he joined in with the debate that it was the wrong thing to do, but at the time he said that he could not help it. He said that having left his status as chairman he felt his control of the meeting disappear like it was "a solid thing turning to gas". His lesson was that he would not allow it to happen again.

Danny introduced the crew to the subject of the meeting and asked the assistant driller, Eddie, to talk us through the timeline of the operation. As usual he asked anyone who had anything to offer to interject whenever they thought it was appropriate. One or two points were made and a minor amendment was being proposed when Mike who had thus far been silent interrupted with the comment that "Your plan is rubbish, this is the way we are going to do it". I could see him settling down in his chair for a long diatribe. He had been deprived of his audience for too long, and was going to enjoy this.

But before he got too comfortable Danny said, "I'm sorry Mike, Eddie is speaking. I'll come back to you when he is finished." I was biting the carpet to keep a straight face but Danny was serious. Eddie finished and Danny turned to Mike with his apology, "OK Mike what was your point?" This time Mike didn't try to take over. Instead he made his point and explained his logic to the meeting, all of whom were listening, then an amazing thing happened.

Mike listened to his own argument and realised that Eddie's idea was better than his. He voiced these thoughts out loud to the meeting and asked for any other comments. The meeting agreed with him that Eddie's idea was better, and Danny thanked Eddie for his input.

Mike was fairly quiet for the rest of the meeting but I could see him thinking furiously, "What is going on here?" I still wasn't sure which way the coin was going to land. Was Mike going to take part or had Danny's treatment of him been too brutal?

After the meeting Mike asked me to bring the amended plan to him so that he could see the changes before it was put into operation. He studied it for a while then asked if I could send it to town so that they could see 'Our Changes'. When he said "Our Changes" I knew that Mike was back on the team.

I was quietly pleased about the way the meeting had turned out. It had proved to be a major turning point in more ways than one.

My conversations with Eddie had always been good fun and never about work. I felt that Eddie knew what I was trying to do and was not very interested, but I did not want to push him away by trying to sell the process too hard. At this meeting Eddie had experienced something so different from his usual encounters with the Company man that I was sure the seed had been sown. I was sure that the nature of my conversations with Eddie would soon be changing.

One of the ways to engage people on the road to ownership is to provide feedback for them. I always looked for ways to encourage other people to give feedback. Having feedback from the boss which is not negative is a very rare thing and yet easy to provide. The Breaking the Mould Process kick-starts that feedback loop.

The process collects ideas and experience from the workforce at debriefing sessions. At these sessions I recorded what the crew thought went well and what they thought could have been better. From these comments I created lessons.

"These are things we want to repeat and changes we would like to make to improve our work". The ideas are then presented to the managers for action from whom only two responses are allowed. "Yes we will do that", with a date for it to be actioned, and "No we are not going to do that", with a reason.

Both of these answers are powerful positive feedback. The crewmember that receives the "No" answer, with a reason why not, is every bit as pleased as the man who gets the "Yes" answer. It gives him respect and tells him that someone is paying attention.

Having artificially seeded the feedback loop it starts to gather momentum. The managers get value from the ideas and improvements and the crew take pride in the fact that their ideas are being listened to by the management. That never happened before.

The goal here is ownership, people taking personal responsibility for themselves, for their own safety and for their own performance. In the collection of ideas, I found that there are a number of distinct stages to go through on the road to ownership, bearing in mind that individuals will take different times to reach each of the stages. Nothing can be done to speed up the process except to continue to seed it by collecting ideas and obtaining feedback.

At first there is the seeding process where the debriefing sessions are organised and ideas collected. Nobody at this stage is willing to offer anything and finding the ideas can be difficult. In this instance due to the crews' history with consultants I found there was considerable peer pressure not to offer anything. As feedback is received and the crew see that no harm is being done, the process of collecting becomes easier and the debriefing meeting can be turned over to the control of the crew.

At some point there is a key moment that I always look for. Until now all the ideas have been solicited. The crew have been responding to direct enquiry. The key moment is when the first idea comes unsolicited. Such was the atmosphere on this platform at the beginning of the project that the first unsolicited idea did not come until the project had been running for nearly six months.

Davey, one of the assistant drillers was the first person to offer a suggestion. He came into the drilling office in the middle of the afternoon when he was fairly sure that it would be quiet. He sidled up to my desk and looking left and right in a furtive way spoke in very short sentences, pausing between them to glance right and left as if making sure that he wasn't overheard. He reminded me of Flash Harry, George Cole's character, in St Trinian's.

Davey told me about his idea to solve a problem with the hydraulic jacks which were used to skid the drilling rig. I wrote it down and solemnly looking left then right, I thanked him for his idea. Again Davey checked the coast was clear before he answered, "That's OK, don't mention it," and with a final check around the room he said, "See ya!" and for a sixteen stone Aberdonian did what I thought was an amazing impression of Flash Harry as he walked away from the office and round the corner.

This was the indicator that someone had taken the first step towards ownership. It had taken a long time.

Stage one is as I described with this crew, every idea has to be wrung from them like drops of blood from a stone, it takes a lot of energy and there is little reward.

Stage two starts to become a little easier when the ideas begin to come in on their own, achingly slowly at first then gradually faster. At the same time the debriefing meeting becomes easier until my only function was to coach the chairman then sit back in the meeting and record any ideas for improvement or lessons that came up.

These first two stages have a common theme. They both have the effect of reporting ideas for someone else to action. At this point it is important to maintain this theme. If someone brings an idea and is told to go and sort it out himself he will stop bringing ideas.

For a lot of managers this is a very effective strategy for reducing their workload. If they tell someone to go away and sort it himself, and he doesn't, the manager can then blame him with a clear conscience because the manager told him quite clearly. In his eyes the failure belongs to the individual and not to the manager. The fact that he will get no more suggestions for improvement brought to him is a happy bonus for the manager who believes that he will then have less work to do.

Alternatively the manager can encourage his team by making things happen, helping others to support ideas, and investing time in the originator so that he understands that his ideas are valued and are being actioned. Most importantly he can give feedback to each individual. As we said earlier, "Yes we are going ahead with this idea, thank you", or, "No we are not going to implement your idea, because....."

"No" and "because", gives just as much respect as "yes". It is being ignored that hurts.

What I found after the first two stages towards ownership have been negotiated was that some individuals would start to move to stage three. Instead of the debriefing being a forum for 'Things that should be done' I found myself recording things that had already been done.

A roughneck told me, "We needed a new pipe wiper but when I asked the stores man he told me there was a two week minimum wait. I found a piece of old air hose and that works a treat so we don't have to order wipers any more"

I recorded the fact that it had been done next to the roughneck's name to make sure that he was given the credit for the idea.

From here some members of the crew move into stage four. This is where they have been heading for a year or sometimes more. This is when I start to see the crews exhibiting real ownership. Stage four is when a crew member has an idea and doesn't even think about writing it down he just does it. He is his own man, he looks at what he is doing then takes that extra step to make it better, because he wants to.

I went up to the rig floor one day late in the project to shoot the breeze with the driller. They had finished laying out pipe in the morning and things had quietened down for a while.

I was walking towards the pipe setback area where the drill pipe was normally kept vertically in the derrick. I was looking around to see where the driller could be, when I tripped but didn't fall. There was something there which had not been before. I recovered and looking down saw that the whole of the setback area had been edged with pieces of five centimetre angle iron bolted to the deck.This formed in effect a bund (a low retaining wall) around the area. I was studying this, puzzled because I was sure it had not been there the day before.

Eddie came around the corner of the doghouse with a pot of yellow paint in his hand, he was clearly just about to use it to paint the bund. There was no one else on the drill floor and he bounded over to me with the expression of an excited child. He looked like something that Jim Henson wished he could have created.

He came up to me with an insane smile, which would have easily got Jim Henson a second and third series. He said, "I've got it, I have finally got it, I know what you have been doing all along, I have finally got it."

Eddie was the one who had so far been allowing the changes to pass him by. I was not sure what Eddie had actually got. I asked Eddie to take me through what he thought he had, and perhaps if he could smile a bit less while he told his story that would be good too.

He began by telling me what I already knew. He'd seen consultants come and he'd seen them go. "When they went you just had to wait a couple of weeks to find out who had been given the sack then you carried on as before. Nothing else ever changed. That was the way that things were."

Eddie's curiosity was aroused when I stuck around. He knew that nobody would be sacked until I left so every day I was there was a bonus, but he saw no signs of any reports being compiled either, only questions about what he needed to improve his job.

Then things started to appear on the rig which had been asked for by the crew. For the most part they had been asked for years before and nothing had ever happened; now they were here; a new winch, a chemical injection unit, a water boiler for the tearoom. Where was the catch? You never get anything for nothing. Eddie went with the flow and kept his eyes open. He even started to put a few ideas of his own forward to find out what was going on and he still could not figure out what was the catch, because there had to be one.

That morning as the last joints of pipe had been laid out Eddie looked at the setback area, bare of pipe, and thought that now would probably be a good time for someone to put a bund round the area.

The drill pipe in use is filled with oil based drilling mud. It looks like mud and that is what it is, except that instead of water the base liquid in this mud was diesel oil. When the drill pipe is pulled out of the hole it is stacked vertically in the setback area and the mud runs down the inside of the pipe and pools on the deck. Being mud the setback area is the last place it wants to stay. Despite the best efforts of the roughnecks the mud migrates to every corner of the drill floor where it permeates everything and very quickly boots, coveralls, gloves and of course the deck is covered in this extremely slippery and sticky mud. This makes tripping pipe (running the pipe in or out) quite an unpleasant and potentially dangerous experience.

Eddie had always had an idea that a bund would solve the problem. The mud would stay in that corner of the drill floor then a small pump would be used to take it out straight to the drains tank.

However the rig was twenty five years old, Eddie had been there ten years and nothing had ever been done. Or, as Eddie saw it now, for ten years he had done nothing.

That was Eddie's revelation. He had stopped thinking that someone else should do something about the bund and realised that he was someone and there was no reason why he could not do it right now.

So he did, and after twenty five years it was accomplished.

Eddie had achieved it.

He told me that he now understood that he had been his own worst enemy. "The only thing stopping us from taking responsibility is ourselves."

I wanted to disagree and suggest that the mangers and supervisors who had denied him that responsibility should take the blame but Eddie's story and his thanks were becoming a bit too emotional and the last place I wanted to be seen to shed a tear was on the rig floor.

I made my excuses and left. Eddie set about painting his new bund bright yellow, so that no one else would trip over it.

Eddie never spoke of that day again but I was always wary where I put my feet and every so often I would come across little things that had the unmistakable stamp of one of Eddie's projects. Whenever we met now Eddie had a new smile about him that an English dog breeder would have died for.

I continued working on that platform for another three months. Life became easier. There were one or two others who reached stage four though none as dramatically as Eddie. The rest of the crews were strung out between stages one and three, and some would change with the wind. People are like that, there are no rules, only faith in the direction in which we are travelling.

By defining the different behaviour of people through the stages to empowerment I was able to measure the progress of the crews towards real ownership.

I counted the number of lessons which I gathered in each of the four ways :

1. Lessons which I learned by asking the crews what they thought.

2. Lessons which the crew brought to me without prompting.

3. Facts which were reported historically, they had already been done.

4. Deeds which were done without any reference to the process.

The changing proportions while having no basis in science allowed me to see changes in behaviour and importantly, let the client see those changes too.

Tracking these changes was not an attempt to get everybody up to Eddie's level. It was an acknowledgement of the different lengths of time it takes for individuals to decide where they are going to go.

I never found a way to hurry the process along, everyone finds their own level in their own time. The only result of trying to hurry people to a conclusion was to build up a resistance that either slowed the change process down or stopped it dead.

What I learned from Eddie and Mike was the patience to allow people to make up their own minds, and more importantly, the futility of trying to make their minds up for them.

Chapter 12

Who Moved My Cheesecake?

On an oil rig in the middle of the North Sea there is never much incentive to keep fit and it is very easy to fall into a cycle of sloth. Sleep, work, eat, sleep, and on energetic days perhaps a few laps of the TV remote control before sleep.

This is the offshore trap that many were beginning to realise was not very good for the long-term maintenance of their bodies.

The rig operators realised the same thing and with a commendable sense of responsibility sponsored ideas to break the cycle and encourage people to take better care of themselves during their time offshore.

On one rig the crews had responded to the operators' initiative by starting a wellness competition.

Teams of three entered the competition and were given full medicals to ascertain percentage body fat, respiration efficiency, cardiovascular function, weight etc.

Once registered the teams commenced their various regimes of diet and exercise and were given points towards a final total to measure changes in lifestyle and reflect the value of exercise taken.

There was one point for every mile on the stationary cycle, two points for every mile on the running machine and three for every mile rowed.

The team with the highest total each month were awarded a prize.

The gym was busy all day with people recording points towards their personal wellness goals.

They smiled through gritted teeth as they forced their unaccustomed bodies to sweat and strain at a point in their lives when their bodies were thinking, thank goodness we have got rid of that youth stuff; running around, bad skin, hormones etc.

The body was happily slinking towards its personal event horizon, content in the knowledge that the further it sank into the couch the less likely it would be that anyone would notice what a state it was in.

These "dormant" bodies were now being thrashed to within an inch of sanity by their owners who, in addition to putting extra strain on them, also reduced the amount of food which their bodies received.

The result was that the body was even less capable of performing these Herculean exertions than before and equally, it was also less capable of repairing the damage which these exercises caused.

The health sentiment is noble and to be encouraged for all the right reasons but there is another side to the fitness infection which seemed to have gripped so many.

Not everyone had been able to get into a team.

There were people who worked alone and didn't have two colleagues to join in a team. There were those who realised quite sensibly that there could be real danger in asking their heart to do any more than the resting pulse rate that has served so well for the last twenty years, and there were those whose list of possible team members was so small (for a variety of reasons, body odour, halitosis, flatulence) that they did not have two friends to rub together to make a team.

However I wasn't worried about these misfits, these social outcasts. For many of them this was the first time that there had been enough cheesecake at lunch. When they left the table there were still meringues in the server.

If the pudding was apple crumble or sticky toffee it was no longer important to get in early because now there was always enough, and the custard never ran out.

Who Moved My Cheesecake?

I took my hat off to these energetic gentlemen who missed lunch to go to the gym. They left more elbow room for me at the table, and there was always more cheesecake in the cold cabinet.

I could always work off the extra weight when I got home on leave, honest!

Chapter 13

Killer Whales, KPIs And Consequences

My senior manager phoned me on the rig one day and casually asked how things were going.

I had been on the rig in the Northern North Sea for some time implementing the Breaking the Mould process. The implementation by that time was beginning to mature and my focus was changing to one of coaching the managers in the skills and techniques they would need to continue to realise their new levels of performance when I left.

My first thought was, how are things going? I had been there for a long time. Had I become part of the status quo which all those months ago I had undertaken to change?

I told my manager that I had been continuing the coaching sessions with the supervisors. He naturally enough was curious to know what it was that had been discussed and I replied glibly, "Killer Whales, KPI's and Consequences."

In retrospect this was hardly a fair thing to do to a colleague who was after all doing his best, I thought I should explain.

When I arrived on the platform my brief was to implement the Performance Improvement Process for the drilling team. The concept of coaching was in its infancy. Keen to explore this new idea I began to experiment with ways that I could implement a coaching programme on the rig.

Coaching itself is a familiar word which is accepted without further qualification because we believe that we know what it means. However the context in which the word is familiar is the sports pavilion, not the business arena, in which it is now commonly being used.

In general we have a fairly sophisticated idea already of the work of the sports coach.

The coach takes a fit, strong well motivated person and he allows that athlete to realise the full potential of his or her body. The athlete is already strong. The coach provides the focus, technique and energy to an already prepared body. This allows the athlete to improve.

This idea translates very effectively to the business arena in which the business leader / manager is guided and supported to a new focus, a new understanding of his personal effectiveness and real power.

The model however falls short in reality of the needs of the skilled tradesman who is promoted to a position of authority with no management or leadership skills available to him. All of his working life he has been using the familiar tools to which he was introduced during his apprenticeship. These are the tools which he has used to produce results for which he was paid. His promotion to a supervisory or managerial position puts him in a place where he is no longer allowed to use his old familiar tools. He is in a new position and is expected to produce results without the training or experience to indicate how he might set about it.

In the equivalent situation is the man on the street who finds himself being coached by an athlete. He doesn't even speak the same language.

"What has diet got to do with it?" "What do you mean go for a run?" "What's wrong with the bus?" "Cross training?" "Do you mean learn how to get angry?" "Don't call me overweight!"

There is no reason why the second man cannot become as motivated and effective as the first but it is apparent that some extra work is required to reach the same level. In terms of the athletic relationship the coach would not normally entertain the man in the street. Before he could get into a pure coaching scenario there would have to be an enormous investment in time and effort to help John Doe reach a level where his performance could be attributed to coaching rather than an increased fitness level.

Business Coaches don't have the luxury of being able to pick and choose their trainees, or the level to which they are trained before they meet them. The Business Coach accepts whomsoever he encounters and is prepared to take on the man in the street with the same enthusiasm and the same end in mind as the business athlete who is already up and running.

The business athlete is a person already trained and fit who has the tools he requires, the value added comes from the softer guidance, facilitative and support skills of the coach.

The man in the street, at the opposite end of the spectrum cannot respond to the softer skills because he has yet to learn the language which would allow him to appreciate the concepts.

At the base level there is a man who first wants to know what the word ownership means in his own language before he can consider the relevance of the concept and begin to think about a strategy to create the conditions for it in the workplace.

On an oil rig there is a management structure in the drilling team consisting of skilled engineers whose entire professional lives have been spent learning how to drill wells. Now they were supervisors and managers whose greatest qualification was, in some cases, old age.

They were not business athletes.

The word coaching and the initial narrow definition of the word was not meant to cover the teaching, training and mentoring that has to occur to prepare these managers to reach for the coaching relationship.

I could see that if I stuck to the traditional view of business coaching I would lose the ability to serve this important section of his client base. These tradesmen turned managers constitute the bulk of the supervisors in most industries.

I therefore expanded the offer to the offshore team, including in their expectation the transfer of management concepts, hard skills which would be of immediate value to them during the life of the project.

In this way I showed the client that while I was increasing their immediate short-term value as managers, I was also preparing them for the subsequent one on one coaching relationship which would aid their progress to the next level of performance.

I realised that the whole coaching offer was supported by two groups of skills the 'Soft skills' and the 'Hard skills' :

The Soft skills :

(Predominantly used for the business athlete.)

- Guidance
- Facilitation
- Support

The Hard skills :

(Predominantly used with the man who has no formal business background.)

- Teaching
- Training
- Educating

These two sets of skills are not used exclusively within different client groups. The hard skills still have their place with the business athletes and the softer skills still provide value to the supervisor. Knowing that both were necessary significantly broadens the offer to both groups of managers.

Coaching is initially confusing to the untutored manager because he knows what a coach is but can't see how or why it would apply to him.

I set up a coaching programme for the offshore people which recognised the individuality of the participants. The programme suggested themes to explore and models which could make the exploration easier. In this way I was able to establish progress and importantly, measure it.

The teaching/training sessions continued in the background as operations allowed, sometimes more frequent sometimes less, but always making measurable progress.

Thus it was that at nine thirty on a cold spring morning in the middle of a gale of Wagnerian proportions I found myself on the phone with my manager delving backwards to the session with my supervisor the previous evening. I was trying to remake the connections between what had been a personal one on one conversation and the coaching process I had been charting.

The man I had been coaching, Paul, had developed in a very traditional way for the offshore industry. With little formal education he started at the bottom and by hard work, lots of application and a good mind he had been promoted to drilling team leader.

For fifteen years he had never stopped learning his trade and as a result of his exceptional technical performance he was promoted to manager, a job for which he had neither trained nor prepared. As a man accustomed to being exceptional he was now acutely aware of his complete lack of tools to help him in his new job, facing the prospect that as a manager he would probably be judged mediocre for the first time in his life.

I remembered the Peter Principle from the seventies. While we are good at our work and therefore enjoy it, we can be confident of a steady rise through our chosen field. The rise continues until we find ourselves promoted into a position for which we are neither prepared nor suited. At this point our performance suffers and because we are not performing well we are no longer considered for promotion. We are definitely no longer happy. We have been promoted until we reach a position of incompetence, and then we are trapped.

Paul's situation was not unique, and in the offshore industry unfortunately not even rare.

It was to him I had been talking the previous evening and it was that conversation I now had to piece together for my supervisor.

Over the months I had about ten coaching sessions with Paul and as the gaps in his knowledge began to be filled in, his arsenal of tools began to be fleshed out. The teaching sessions began to change their character from one of learning to one of facilitated discussion. The latest had started off with the idea of showing how one of the models we had discussed previously could be found in almost all of the work that I did. The part of the model under discussion was 'Consequences' from the ABC model of Activator, Behaviour, Consequence.

The ABC model describes two ways the manager has of influencing the 'B'. 'B' is the employee or team 'Behaviour' he is trying to influence.

This model defines two ways of controlling behaviour. The first and most favoured method is 'A', the 'Activator".

The Activator is the manager's traditional tool. "Simply tell someone what to do and because I am your superior you will go away and do it until such time as I tell you to stop".

Unfortunately, despite its popularity with managers this is the least effective way of getting someone to do what you want.

Some months ago I had talked with Paul about the Activator as the pointed finger telling someone what to do, the primary effect being to make the person on one end of the finger very angry with the person wagging the other end.

Having been angered the person on the wrong end of the wagging finger will then do their job badly because the Activator driven boss doesn't deserve to have it done well, or they might think of a reason why they can't do it at all, or they will say, "Yes of course, I'll do it right away", then go away and read the paper.

I knew that Paul understood this and I could see the smile of recognition in his eyes from his own brushes with the wrong end of someone else's wagging finger.

We had talked about 'B', 'Behaviour', at length. We talked about Paul's function as a manager being to influence people and how that influence affected performance. Logically, how that influence could be used to improve performance.

As a manager could Paul do something to influence the Behaviour of his team without the negative effects we had discussed?

Paul talked about his change in attitude, how he felt personally when people stopped telling him what to do and instead asked him for his ideas or praised him for his effort.

Now we were cooking, this was what I wanted to hear.

Now I was ready to take the idea of the ABC model onto the rig floor to explore how it was being used and whether there were any opportunities we might find to develop it.

Specifically, how the power of the positive consequence could be applied practically to help change behaviour.

Paul had grasped the principle firmly enough and had included a commitment in his personal development contract to take time out every day to give quality time to a different one of his men. It is not until you understand how full his day was already that it is possible to appreciate the tremendous self-discipline and energy that he had to invest in the maintenance of that commitment.

When I asked Paul to figure out what he did to provide a positive consequence to his team, after a bit of head scratching the light bulb started to glow and Paul told me, "The Weekly Safety Award". The rig was running a safety scheme in which safety suggestions were recorded on cards and handed to the supervisors for collation.

There was however a problem with falling numbers as interest in the scheme and therefore numbers of suggestions fell. This led to the numbers of cards written assuming a higher and higher profile at the daily briefings.

The phrase, 'You must fill in more safety cards' had become a daily part of the pre-job briefing.

The more that the crews were told to fill the cards in the more they resisted until the numbers were being kept up by only one or two people in each crew, while the rest of the crew members completely ignored the scheme.

The supervisors had been spending their time telling the crews to fill the cards in. This Paul agreed was an Activator. He was telling them what to do.

After some discussion about the power of positive consequences Paul made a conscious decision to back off from this negative approach and the weekly safety award was instituted. The weekly award was available to everyone, the actual award was not of great value but the possibility of winning provided a positive consequence for every one who wrote a card. Without realising it the numbers of cards written ceased to be an issue and by regularly publishing the numbers submitted, it soon became apparent that his crews were, per capita, the most prolific contributors to the safety scheme on the platform.

"OK," I said, "We are encouraging people to make safety suggestions by giving a positive consequence. What else?"

Paul said that he also understood that the weekly News Letter, published onboard, was deliberately filled with positive consequences for all of the crew. Their efforts were recognised and praised every week. He also understood the idea that providing feedback to an individual was a positive consequence and that every improvement idea collected from the crew, whatever its practical merits, was also an opportunity to provide a positive consequence - which would in turn encourage the production of more improvement suggestions.

Each idea submitted was assessed and whether implemented or not the result of its consideration would always be fed back to the individual who generated the idea. Each originator received positive feedback for their idea. Thus even if their idea was flawed the feedback which was received encouraged the submission of more ideas for improvement.

This led the conversation round to KPIs and their value as a positive consequence.

KPI's are key performance indicators. They are the bottom line measures of success. If your function is to produce a target number of widgets during a day then that number is your KPI. Most targets are composed of a number of elements upon which they are also conditional. The energy costs to produce each widget could be a KPI, as could the timelines of delivery of raw materials, completion of orders or unit failure rate.

Paul, as an engineer, had been trained that numbers were right and good but that when they were turned into times or targets by managers they became awful things that gave your manager an excuse to shout at you for failing to achieve. They had no place in his world and he had learned they should be avoided at all costs.

This revelation hijacked the session and we spent a good deal of time examining why he had this view of KPI's.

The answer simply was that Paul's only experience of KPIs was exactly as described. An arbitrary set of numbers imposed on him by a faceless manager. They were always difficult to achieve, he had stopped caring whether he did or did not achieve them because the consequence was always the same. If he didn't reach his target he was shouted at and even if he did achieve his goal he was still shouted at, only the subject was different.

He told me that he had been running casing as a roughneck and the KPI set by the office had been twenty four joints an hour. They had been running for a couple of hours when he saw one of the roughnecks talking to the driller. He called the roughneck over after the next joint and was told with a smile that in the last hour they had run twenty-three joints. That made him smile too as he realised that it was the fastest that casing had ever been run on that rig.

Paul said that he stopped daydreaming between joints and started to pay attention to what was going on. Pretty soon he edged over to the doghouse and the driller winked through his smile and said, "Twenty-four". When he turned around everyone on the floor was looking at him and when he gave the thumbs up there were smiles and thumbs up all round.

The next hour was like clockwork; no rush, just a well-oiled machine. At the end nobody went to the driller, they just turned to look at him and everybody knew the result. The driller looked at his recorder and there it was, twenty-five joints in the last hour, for the first time ever.

The Toolpusher at the time had a repeater of the recorder in his office and came up to the rig floor to see what was going on. On his way up to the rig floor he put his hand in some grease which had found its way onto the handrail. He went straight to the driller with the grease and asked him what sort of a drill floor he thought he was running.

Paul was the man sent to clean off the grease, and when he came back the KPI was never mentioned again. The performance never again exceeded twenty joints per hour. The cost of the Toolpusher's behaviour was five joints an hour. His behaviour instantly reduced performance by twenty percent, and he thought he was doing a good job!

"KPI's?" Paul said, "You can stick them."

"Hold on a minute," I said, "Whose KPI do you want to stick, the one that was set at twenty four by the office that was so impossible, or the KPI of twenty five that you yourselves had set and were so confident of achieving that you did not even have to check the recorder?"

This was an angle that Paul had not previously considered.

The discussion eventually came to the conclusion that it was good to set your own targets and because they were your own you could take pride in their achievement. If they were set for you it was just someone else on your back telling you what to do.

This was worth an instant 20% difference in performance. If someone sets a target for you it is an 'Activator'. If you can set your own target then its achievement became a positive 'Consequence'.

I was prepared to call it a night by then because we had come a long way in a short time and I didn't want to run the risk of muddying the waters of Paul's understanding. I had already stood up to go when Paul said slowly, "So if I set my own KPI that gives me a positive Consequence because I can take pride in the result, and if someone else sets the KPI then that is an Activator because it is just another way of telling me what to do."

"Good, does that feel right to you?" I sat down again wondering how he was going to conclude the session without losing his focus on these key building blocks.

Paul did not reply, I could see he was thinking hard.

A small familiar voice coming from just under where my hair used to be told me to shut up and see what happened. The voice had never been wrong in the past so I waited.

We sat on, the phone didn't ring, the tannoy system was silent and nobody interrupted to ask for Paul's signature.

Then Paul said, "Can I still give someone a good bollocking?"

I nearly smiled but just in time realised that Paul was being perfectly serious. This was the one management tool with which he was completely happy, he was now worried that the only thing that he thought he could count on was being taken away.

I asked him why he would want to give anyone a bollocking. Paul thought about this just long enough to confirm that he probably did enjoy it, then admitted that it did not really make sense to do it at all but how else would you shift someone back on track.

I asked him what would be classed as a successful bollocking. Paul was in his element here and he drew breath.

" It is when you leave the person in no doubt about what they have done wrong. Don't let them say anything, they will just try to make excuses.

127

You tell them exactly what will happen if they ever screw up again and when they leave they are so scared they will never dream of doing it again".

"Don't get me wrong" he said, "You don't have to shout, it's all in the tone of voice and it is really great to end with something like, "Is that clear?" If they don't say anything you can say it again but a bit louder. "Is that clear?" It is really effective."

I wanted to go but I couldn't leave it like that. I asked Paul if he could tell me what his recent experience had taught him about changing people's behaviour. Paul didn't have to think for very long before he looked up, "Yes, yes, I know all that stuff about giving positive consequences to encourage and support the correct behaviours but I still have to give people bollockings, it's my job."

I said, "If you are telling me that it is written into your contract of employment that you have to do this then good luck to you but I have to ask, where is the positive experience for the person on the receiving end? "You prejudge, you don't listen, you bully and threaten, and all that achieves is to make you feel good.

"Let us just consider what you are assuming about that person when you deliver your tirade. The first assumption is that the person is guilty of wanton failure. By telling him not to do it again you are assuming that he did it deliberately and that it was in his power to stop doing it. If he did do it deliberately he will not stop just because you tell him to. However, if we can accept a basic truth about people that they all want to do a good job, we have to assume that the act or omission was not deliberate."

I went on, "In this case you are starting your meeting with someone who knows exactly what he has done wrong, is apologetic and perhaps has a couple of ideas that could stop others making the same mistake.

"At the end of the meeting you have accused him of deliberately undermining the team, you have refused to listen to him and you have used your position of authority to bully him in the certain knowledge that he can't hit you back.

"If he made another mistake do you think that he would come to you and admit it after you had treated him like that?" Paul had to admit, "Probably not."

I continued, "Now suppose that the next mistake he made was to drop a spanner down the well you were drilling and he didn't tell you. You go back in to the well with a drill bit, you start drilling and no progress is made. You can't see what is happening down the well, it may take a couple of days to figure out what has happened. The cost of that mistake could be easily more than a million pounds and all because he didn't tell you what he had done. If on the other hand he told you that he had dropped the spanner, the recovery would have started straight away and may have cost as little as fifty thousand pounds. That makes the cost of giving him a bollocking nine hundred and fifty thousand pounds.

Is that a price you want to pay?"

Paul was quiet, he had clearly never thought of the effect of his bollockings in this way before. To break the silence, I asked him how he would deliver a bollocking to a killer whale.

Paul had not expected the question so I explained.

"If you want a killer whale to jump out of the water and it doesn't, how would you deal with it? Withhold food? Shout at it? Stop its playtime? Whatever you do you are going to make it angry. You don't have to be a trainer of large carnivorous mammals to know that when they are angry, or hungry, it is a good idea to stay away from them, especially if you are the one who made them angry".

That broke the tension but we were still dealing with a live issue. Shouting at someone was the only way that Paul knew to deal with failure. Unless he could see an alternative he was going to remain unconvinced. It had been a long session and we had covered some important ground so I did not want to compromise that progress by starting something fresh.

We had covered coaching, the different needs of a manager trained and familiar with management tools compared to the experience of the technical expert who came to a management position with none of the tools or training to help him. We had talked about the ABC model of Management, the 'Activator', 'Behaviour', 'Consequence'. We had then spent time examining how to provide those positive consequences to the crews on a regular basis, and where some of the things that Paul already did fitted the model, Feedback, Recognition, KPI's.

Paul returned to the question I had left him with, "How do you encourage a killer whale to jump twenty feet into the air, and enjoy it?"

I told him, "It is as easy as ABC.

"Killer whales are very tactile. They enjoy being petted and having attention in much the same way that humans do. The trainer simply puts a rope across the tank under the water. When the whale goes under the rope his behaviour is ignored, when he goes over the rope the trainer will make a fuss of him. It takes very little time for the whale to realise that he has a choice to make when he sees the rope. Either go under it or go over. Going under, nothing happens, going over results in petting and perhaps a fish. The whale chooses to go over the rope and the trainer starts to raise the level of the rope until the whale chooses to leap out of the water to get over the rope.

No shouting required, just a positive consequence for making the right choice.

Chapter 14

Going To Work In The Orinoco

The Orinoco River empties itself into the eastern end of the Caribbean at a point directly south of Trinidad. Going upstream the river goes south then slowly turns towards the west, encircling half of Venezuela until it disappears into the Andes.

In the early sixties the North Americans had been drilling in the Orinoco and had made substantial discoveries in the river delta. They had exploited the site until it became uneconomic to produce any more oil and the field was shut down. In the late seventies the Venezuelan government had had enough of the Americans liberating all their oil. They declared that the whole of the petrochemical industry had been nationalised and threw the North Americans out.

There followed a period of isolationism in which all foreigners were seen to be exploiters of Venezuelan mineral wealth and for a long time the country played its cards very close to its chest. After a while their xenophobia began to die down and foreign expertise gradually began to filter back into the country.

Since the North Americans had first drilled in the Orinoco River, drilling technology had moved on a great deal and what was deemed uneconomic thirty five years ago was now easily achievable.

So it was that a client I had worked with in Europe invited me to come down to Venezuela to help with their drilling operation in the Orinoco River. This sounded like good fun so before I knew what was happening I was struggling through Caracas airport heading for the domestic terminal and a flight for Maturin.

Maturin was the Houston of Eastern Venezuela and from there I was due to catch the Oilfield flight out to Pedernales on the Orinoco River. I arrived and soon tied up with the assorted North Americans and Europeans who were also waiting for the plane.

Breaking The Mould

The flight was not announced but like the swallows' urge to migrate everyone seemed to wander in the same direction at the same time and suddenly we were checked in. It was all a bit confusing, having checked in and therefore lost my bags I expected to have a clear instruction about where to go or what to do next, but instead I was still milling around with the others in the same place. Nobody else seemed any the wiser so I decided to buy a cup of coffee on the basis that if I did not we would be waiting for ever. But having bought it, when it was too hot to drink quickly, I knew from Murphy's Law that we would be summoned to board immediately. It seemed to be a good investment in the reverse use of 'Murphy's Law'.

Murphy's Law says that the toast will always land butter side down, and an extension is that if you are waiting for a plane it will always start boarding when you go to buy a coffee. The reverse use of the Law is to understand that the boarding of the plane does not depend on time. If Murphy's Law is true, and we all know that it is, then boarding the plane depends on you going to buy a cup of coffee and not on the passage of time. Logically, if you want the plane to start boarding, go and buy a cup of coffee. It is remarkable how often it works.

As the coffee shop was about fifteen metres away on the other side of the ticket counter, I wandered over and bought my coffee. I was sorting through my loose change to get rid of as much as possible before leaving, when, glancing in the direction of the milling group, I saw that they had all disappeared.

I couldn't believe it, Murphy's Law had worked again. I pulled out a one hundred Bolivar note and picking up the hot coffee I set off to find my new companions.

When I arrived at the check in I could see no sign of anyone but there was a wide corridor which compared to the bustle in the rest of the airport felt as if it had recently emptied. I set off at a moderate pace trying not to burn myself with the coffee as it sloshed out of the cup at every step. There was a right-angled bend in the corridor going around to the left. As I reached the corner I could see the runway through the glass doors at the end. I did not seem to be spilling quite so much coffee now but looking back could see that a large quantity had already escaped from the cup and was marking the way I had come quite effectively.

Through the doors I was just in time to catch sight of some movement to the left. I ran towards the corner and round it saw the last two passengers making their way up the folding stairs into the aircraft.

I am not an expert on aeroplanes. I think I could probably recognise a Boeing Seven-Four-Seven in the right light but I had no idea what it was that I was stepping into now. I was just grateful that I did not have any more time to inspect the outside of the plane, especially as the fleeting glimpse of scarred paint, large carbon deposits under the wings, battered propellers, a row of misty Plexiglas windows and myriads of bare rivets which had once so obviously been painted, worried me. The less I saw of the outside of the plane the more comfortable I knew I would feel.

There were twenty seats inside, in two rows of ten with the aisle between. I sat in the last vacant seat at the back and busied myself with the seat belt. It worked but handling it and the buckle, worn and shiny at the edges, put me in mind of buying a car. Even if it looked wonderful from the outside you had to be suspicious of what was under the hood if the passenger compartment was as worn out as that.

I was having some trouble trying to reach the belt with one hand and was on the point of putting the coffee down on the deck in the aisle, there were no tables, when a friendly voice from across the aisle offered to take the coffee while I sorted it out. The belt did not take long to fasten and as I took the coffee back my new friend introduced himself as Kurt from Omaha. He guessed that this was my first time out and took it upon himself to fill me in on a few details of the trip.

Between Maturin and the Orinoco was the jungle. (This was delivered in Kurt's best tour guide voice.) There were no roads and no people to speak of. The flight would take about an hour and a half, if everything went well. If it didn't go well we stood no chance of surviving a landing in the jungle. If by some miracle we did survive the impact we would never escape from the jungle and nobody else could get in to rescue us. With that comforting thought Kurt shifted his chewing tobacco to the more comfortable non-speaking position in his mouth and pulled his baseball cap down over his eyes. I turned to look out of my window but it was too small and the Plexiglas in the upper half was starred so that it would have been difficult to see anything anyway.

I was just thinking of doing the same as Kurt when the plane started to wobble in a very disconcerting way. I realised that the pilots were starting up the engines. The vibration got steadily worse then, as the first engine caught and fired. It seemed to die away to be replaced by a sensation very much like using a hammer drill on a tin shed. This seemed to be what the pilot was aiming for, the perfect balance between tooth jarring vibration, and noise.

Before I got used to the first engine I could feel the plane shaking again as the pilot started to spin up the second engine. I could see the propeller turning from my window. After spinning for a while the engine seemed to be in no hurry to fire and soon the propeller was slowing down again, throwing in a couple of last big wobbles to the plane like the washing machine just before it stops when all the wet towels have bunched together on one side.

Well that was that, I thought. A night in Maturin, a few beers then out again tomorrow for another try. I sat up waiting for the word to get off but noticed that no one else had moved. Kurt was still in his 'baseball cap over the eyes' attitude, as were a few of the others, and nobody was paying the slightest attention. After a few minutes one of the pilots emerged from a small hatch at the front of the plane with an adjustable spanner.

He walked round to the engine which I could just see out of the window. The pilot lifted the engine cover, folded it back like the hood of a vintage car and stuck both arms and his head inside. I did not like the idea of repairs at the side of the runway but at least the pilot looked as if he knew what he was doing. Unscrewing something with the spanner he pulled it out and started to blow in it. He did this several times then he held another small pipe outside the cowling and what I could only assume was fuel started to trickle slowly out onto the runway. The pilot gave it a few seconds then unhurriedly put it back inside and started to screw it up with the wrench. I watched in amazement as he came out and gave a thumbs up to the other pilot.

He stepped back a little and the propeller began to turn. This time it caught almost immediately and a huge black cloud erupted from the back of the engine, gradually diminishing as the revs grew higher. As the engine gathered speed its din seemed to harmonise with that of the already running engine so that with both of them running it actually seemed more comfortable than with just one.

I glanced over at Kurt who still hadn't moved. He must have caught my movement, pausing only to shift his tobacco over to the other side of his mouth he said, "Same thing every time, don't know why they don't get it fixed, won't be long now. See you later," and sliding his tobacco back he closed his eyes.

I didn't have long to wait and we were soon barrelling down the runway. The noise was horrendous and as we picked up speed the plane started to shimmy from side to side. I had a fairly strong stomach but I could not figure out which part of the ancient plane could be causing this particular motion and was beginning to get worried again. Glancing over at Kurt who had not moved, I had to assume that whatever the plane was doing it was normal and tried hard not to worry, it was difficult.

Lifting off from the runway was delirious, most of the vibration stopped, the plane straightened up and it began to feel as if we would make it to the Orinoco. I had my face pressed to the clear part of the window as we rose, trying to take in as much as possible of the city of Maturin. Unfortunately the airport was to the east of the city and we were heading east. All I saw were a few adobe huts with scrub filled yards which very quickly gave way to scrub filled countryside with no adobe.

Within a few minutes the slightly brown, dry looking scrub started to fill with a richer green and a few minutes after that there was no doubt that this was the jungle that Kurt had been talking about. From a height it was

135

a beautiful light green, almost fluorescent, cut from time to time with the flash of the sun against the water in amongst the trees. I could not understand why Kurt in his morale-boosting introduction to Oilfield Airways had failed to mention the fact that under the impenetrable jungle was a swamp. I felt cheated. I made a mental note to mention it to Kurt when we landed.

Soon the novelty of seeing green everywhere began to pall and I made myself as comfortable as I could to try and catch a little sleep. I wasn't aware of having slept but was suddenly alert to the fact that the engine note had changed. As I listened I could hear one engine winding down with a finality which said, "I am not having a rest, this is me stopping for good."

My first reaction was to look across at Kurt, who was in exactly the same position as before, looking down the length of the cabin I still seemed to be the only one who had noticed anything. The view out of the window was predictably green so I fixed my attention on what I could see of the pilots through the cockpit curtain. There did not seem to be any rush so I thought that if nobody else was worried it was a bit foolish to waste a good panic that might come in handy later on.

There was a minute or two of calm organisation behind the pilots' curtain then the plane started to dive towards the jungle. By now I was so used to the idea that everybody else had seen this all before that I turned my attention to the tree canopy below and wondered how close we would get to it. The trees were getting closer and I was beginning to look for the belch of black smoke from the engine that would signal the end of our descent.

No smoke appeared. The remaining engine was screaming and the plane started to pull up. I almost didn't hear Kurt when he said, "That's strange, this usually does it."

I turned towards him but he hadn't moved. The only sign that he had spoken was the lump of tobacco under his lip sliding back to the 'Off' position.

We were climbing fairly steeply now, the plane gave a lurch and a very quiet calm descended on the cabin, no engine noise at all. A familiar voice behind me said, "Now that is interesting," and looking back over my shoulder I could see that Kurt was awake. Now I was worried. The plane seemed to lose its momentum very quickly and flopped over until it was nose down and starting to pick up speed again.

At first it was deadly quiet then the noise of the air whistling past the fuselage seemed to grow in the silence until I was sure that even if I spoke nobody would hear my voice. Kurt was sitting up now alternating his glance between the cockpit and the jungle below. I was strangely reassured. Now that Kurt had taken over the worrying I felt I could concentrate on the rapidly approaching forest canopy. I could make out individual trees by the time the big black cloud finally blossomed under the wing and with no time for finesse the nose was pointed back up to the sky and the one sick engine was given the gun.

Finally back to what I assumed to be cruising altitude the throttle was backed off fractionally. The din of the single engine screaming at the top of its voice was still too much for ordinary conversation. The plane levelled out and for the next few minutes there were sporadic attempts to start the other engine until finally it coughed a couple of times then roared enthusiastically into life as if it had just nipped out for a few minutes and didn't think that anyone would have noticed.

I must have fallen asleep because the next thing I knew I was waking up as the plane began a steep banking turn. I looked quickly across at Kurt. He had gone back to his usual position and was still asleep so I assumed that we had arrived. I looked out of the window and as the turn grew steeper the Orinoco river came into view flashing hugely silver against the impossible green of the forest.

The plane had lost a lot of height already so I could make out the wooden huts built out over the river and watched as a small boy came rushing out of one of the huts to leap into the river just before it disappeared under the wing.

I was craning my head round to try to see the boy surface when the bank of the river seemed to erupt with a colour so vivid it was startling. I could not tell what was going on at first then realised they were pink flamingos, except that these were scarlet. They had been fishing in the mud at the edge of the river and had risen with the approach of the plane. I watched them until they too vanished behind the plane. What a sight! I had half a mind to wake Kurt but was sure he would have seen it before.

Looking ahead through the cockpit I saw that the plane was heading for a runway. I was not aware of any significant drop in speed and I could see out of the window that the wheels were not down. I was faced with a choice. Clearly there was a need for wheels at some point in the landing.

I knew this because I had seen them in Maturin and they had definitely been down. On the other hand if I stood up now to walk the length of the plane and tell the pilots that the wheels were not down and if for some reason they already knew this, if it was part of the plan and if I did not die my life on the rig would be hell because everyone on board would know what I had done.

I took the coward's way out and stayed in my seat, at least if the plane ploughed into the runway we would all be dead and no one would ever know that it was me who had seen that the wheels were not down and did not tell the pilot. The plane banked lower and lined up on the runway, still no wheels, now heading straight down the middle of the runway which had been cut into the jungle at right angles from the edge of the river. We flew lower, almost touching the river then as we crossed the bank both throttles were flung wide open and the plane screamed up the length of the runway at zero feet.

By now it was obvious that there was some method here but the logic still defeated me. At the end of the runway the nose was pulled up sharply and at the same time the plane spun around to the left. It seemed to stand on its wing tip, pivoting around until it was heading back the way it had just come. I looked over at Kurt and waited while he adjusted his tobacco to speak. "M'Alligators" he said then switched back to 'off'.

So eloquent, it was obvious. The alligators crawled out of the river to sun themselves on the tarmac and the easiest way to clear them off the runway was to scare the life out of them by firing an aeroplane full of oilfield workers down the runway. Small wonder there were no flight attendants. Nobody would have believed the attendants if they had explained in the pre-flight safety demonstration what was considered to be normal for this flight. If they had been believed I was sure there was a good chance that half the passengers would not have got on the plane in Maturin.

The plane landed without further incident and the baggage was reclaimed from a pile in the long grass where the baggage carousel would no doubt one day be. The Indian who put the bags down apologised for the length of the grass. He told me they had put two cows onto the runway last month to keep the grass short but both had disappeared. "Look after your bags, Señor, I think there are bad people around".

"Or perhaps good alligators" I thought.

When the plane was coming in to land I had caught a glimpse of the rig on the other side of the river a mile downstream. It looked very odd in a landscape where everything else was the same size and colour, yet here it was, stuck in the river, massive and hugely orange.

Standing by the side of the runway it was hot but not unbearably so, just hot enough for me to realise that moving anywhere with a bag was going to end up a very sweaty experience. We clustered in small groups, and occasionally someone would talk. Kurt said, "Aw wipe," when he got off the plane but now he was sitting with his cap over his eyes against the wall of the shed that had an 'Aduana' (Customs) sign hanging by a single rusty hook. There were no signs or guides. The pilots stayed on the plane and after a few minutes a jeep turned up and dropped off four tired looking guys with their bags. As soon as the last bag was off Kurt, who had become magically animated, threw his bag into the back and climbed in next to the driver.

Three others followed suit and the heavily laden jeep disappeared up the track. In about ten minutes it was back with another four people going home and the process was repeated until in the final jeep I took a seat and was deposited with the others at the end of the jetty. At the other end lay the launch which was waiting to take us all down the river to the rig.

I felt a bit sad to be saying goodbye to the journey, it felt as if it was an entity in itself. I felt ungrateful to have come so far from the West Coast of Scotland to a tiny village of crab fishing Indians on the banks of the Orinoco without being able to spend some time with them. I thought that the village and the people deserved more than a quick glance as I waited for the boat to pull me away back to another world on the other side of the river.

I felt uneasy to be passing these people in their world without being given the opportunity to say hello.

On my next trip to the rig I found a brand new aeroplane in Maturin with a flight attendant, a coffee and a sandwich. As we approached the runway with both engines still working I braced himself mentally for the race down the runway and the pirouette at the end.

Coming in from the river side of the strip I could see the new chain link fence which surrounded the landing field in which I also noted that the grass had been cut. It was disappointing when I felt the wheels go down and we landed on the first pass. The bags still ended up in a pile on the grass but I couldn't help feeling that the journey had lost something by becoming ordinary.

Chapter 15

Rio Orinoco

On the trip to the rig across the river from the landing strip I had time to think about what was happening and to go over the little that I had managed to find out about the job I was coming to do.

The rig I was coming to was fairly new and had been on site for two years. Two years was therefore the average drilling experience of the crews although the Venezuelan drillers had all been brought in from elsewhere and could be expected to have a little more experience.

In addition to the local crews there were North American drillers who were, to honour the local labour agreement, not allowed to drill. They acted as mentors for the crews and all the other contractors were either North American or European.

When I arrived there was a preliminary feeling each other out period when the contractors tried to figure out how much I was going to interfere with them and I tried to figure out where I could give the greatest value.

I was arriving at an ailing project and the clients were keen to have something that they could point to and say that this was why they had employed me. Short term gains are generally the stuff of dreams and textbooks written in the sixties by graduates with stopwatches.

I was aiming to produce sustainable change with a simple beginning, middle and an end which was visible and could be measured. This would allow me to answer the clients' "How is it going?" question with more than just words. They wanted results. That was what they were paying for. During the assessment period I spent a lot of time doing the easiest thing in the world, listening. I had a bag full of consultant's tools and this was always the first one to bring out and the most effective. Just listen.

The contractors were the usual bunch of oilfield professionals whose lives bounce around the globe from rig to rig. Apart from the temperature outside they could be anywhere on the planet. These guys have a job to do, they do it and then they are off to a desert or an ocean in the other hemisphere with the same ease that most of us get in and out of a car.

The North Americans in the drill crew were another matter. They always came back to the same rig and were all extremely busy men. I found that stopping them long enough to have a conversation was very difficult. They were either in the process of shouting at the crew or were on their way somewhere else to do some more shouting.

As an apprentice at sea in the Merchant Navy I had been shouted at, as I was sure that most people had been when they were training. What I remembered was that I didn't like it very much. It made me angry, it made me sullen and uncommunicative and if there was a situation where it was possible that something might get broken, then it generally did (It wasn't my fault!). This of course led to more shouting and more sullen disobedience.

On the occasions when I did get to talk to the North Americans they complained of having to run the crews without touching anything, of crews who were so stupid that they had to be told which way to open a valve (anticlockwise) every time, and of crews who didn't understand the first thing about drilling and never would. They were a tired and disillusioned group of people.

The Indians on the other hand were a lively bunch who were always ready to pass the time of day or have a bit of fun, unless one of the North Americans was near. Then they would be very quiet and only respond to direct orders.

The first thing that struck me about the situation was that the North American drillers who were not allowed to drill, were in fact the busiest people on the rig. The reason for that was that every action that had to be performed in order to drill the well had to be performed by them telling each crew member individually, through sign language, exactly what was required before moving on to explain the next task to the next man in the same way.

There were two reasons why they had to do this. Each time they told a crew member what to do they did not explain why he was doing it. The crew were told what to do without any reference to the system they were using or the effect of what they were doing was having on the overall drilling process (Just, "Open this valve," or "close that valve."). The American would then move on to the next man, very comfortable with himself because he knew that he did not have the time to explain, he was a busy man and his job was telling people what to do.

The other reason that they had to explain every single time which way to turn a valve in order to open or close it was because the Orinoco Indians were playing games with them.

The Indians before the arrival of the rig spent their lives catching crabs, catfish and forty winks whenever the opportunity arose. The North American drillers judged them all as lazy and ignorant, which was evident in the complete absence of respect that they gave the Indians.

The Indians as a result made life as difficult as they could for the Americans. They would deliberately misunderstand instructions, they would ask for everything to be explained twice, they would fail to understand and the drilling would have to stop while a translator was found. The translator would arrive and wink at the crew as he translated an instruction that they had all understood perfectly well the first time around.

The Americans were definitely the busiest people on the rig.

The week after I arrived I was sitting with the mud engineer discussing the system for delivering the drilling mud which lubricated the bit.

Whenever you drill a hole there is material from the hole which has to be removed from it. If a piece of wood is drilled the wood comes out of the hole in a spiral. When we are drilling rock the bit crushes the rock and it comes off the face in small pieces. These cuttings have to be brought back to the surface. This is achieved using a drill string (the lengths of drill pipe when screwed together) of open pipe. There is a hole down the middle through which drilling mud is pumped. The cuttings from the bottom of the well are then picked up in the mud and brought back to the surface between the outside of the drill pipe and the wall of the hole that has been drilled. When the mud reaches the surface it is sent over shaker screens which allow the mud to fall through but catch all of the cuttings.

The mud, now clean, goes back down the well to pick up more cuttings, and the cuttings which have been recovered are sent to a barge from where they are eventually taken upriver to be used, in this instance, as the base for a new road.

This is a closed system with a constant volume of mud which is always circulating. The driller monitors the volume of mud very carefully because it tells him important information about the condition of the well.

If the volume of mud increases it means that something is coming into the well. It may be oil or it may be water or it may be gas. If it is gas the bubble will expand as it rises up the well, when it reaches the surface it can throw the drill pipe out of the hole and blow the rig to pieces. If it ignites the consequences are even more dramatic.

If the volume of mud decreases rapidly then the formation may have started to soak up the mud and it may be necessary to withdraw the string and go back in to cement up the leak. This can be very expensive.

While drilling the American driller had briefed his crew. He told his Venezuelan assistant driller to hang a nut on a piece of string over the circulating tank so that it was touching the surface of the mud. "If the nut stops touching the surface of the mud I want to know immediately". The purpose of this instruction was to indicate to the driller whether the level of mud was rising or falling.

At the shakers the mud engineer had given his instructions to the Indian helping him.

If the flow was too fast the mud would not have time to fall through the shaker screens. It would go back to the mud pumps still carrying pieces of the drilled rock which would then cause damage to the pumps.

The mud engineer's instructions to the Indian were that if the mud started to flow over the back of the screens, i.e. it was flowing too fast, he should close down the valve to restrict the flow.

I was sitting with a cup of coffee in the mud laboratory when with no warning the mud engineer leapt to his feet and flew out of the cabin. I had no idea what was going on so I followed at a more sedate pace to find out what the problem was.

The problem was that the rig had pumped nearly three thousand barrels of mud out of the mud system into the cuttings' barge in the river. The base of this mud was an exotic environmentally friendly vegetable oil that had cost over ninety dollars per barrel. The value of the mud that had been pumped over the side into the barge was over a quarter of a million dollars!

I decided that this was not a good place to be while everyone else was doing the wall of death so I retreated to my own office to wait while everybody calmed down.

After a few days I managed to piece the story together. The formation had been good and the rig was making steady progress. The American driller had become concerned that the hole was not being cleaned properly so he ordered the pump speed to be increased to pick up more of the cuttings, but he did not tell anyone else that he had increased the pump speed.

The increased rate caused the mud to flow over the back of the shakers.

The Venezuelan on the shakers was doing exactly as he had been told. He closed the valve to the shakers.

The mud, now unable to get through to the shakers backed up and started to overflow into the barge in the river.

At about this time, a European mud logger, whose job it was to monitor the mud condition and volume, went to the rig floor and informed the American driller that he appeared to be losing mud. The American driller was busy, as he always was, and he shouted at the mud logger, "Are you sure?"

The mud logger was suitably intimidated and said he would go away and check again. He left the drill floor and went back to his office. It took another fifteen minutes before he found enough courage to return to the drill floor and say that this time he was sure they were losing mud.

By that time a quarter of a million dollars' worth of mud had been pumped into the barge.

The mud engineer when he left the mud laboratory ran straight up to the shakers where he saw the Indian roughneck standing next to the shakers beaming with pride. The roughneck knew that he had been asked to do one thing and he had done it. He was sure that the mud engineer was coming to congratulate him.

The American driller ran down to the circulation tank to find out what the assistant driller was doing. He found him beaming in exactly the same way as the roughneck on the shakers. He had been told to do one thing and he was doing it. As the level of the mud in the tank fell, indicating that they were losing mud, he was carefully letting out more string so that the nut on the end was always in contact with the surface of the mud in the tank.

On the rig we never heard the result of the official enquiry but the incident sparked an indignant reaction from the crew. Although nothing was said they all felt that the blame was being heaped on them for a failure over which they had no control. This led to demands from the crew for training so that they could have more control, and more importantly for them, so that they could understand what it was they were being asked to do.

The reaction from the American drillers was still the same. They had no time to train the crews, and it was the crews' fault anyway because they didn't listen. This was familiar ground for me. "It is not my fault, they did not listen."

So I figured out a new approach. The American drillers were helped to write out a list of all the tasks which the crews had to perform and this list was then given to the crews, who made up a matrix which had each of their names against each task.

Rio Orinoco

Under each task, were three boxes. The boxes were marked :

1. He has been shown how to do this.

2. He has completed the task on his own.

3. He is competent.

The matrix was posted on the rig floor and its purpose explained to the crews. There was a reluctance at first to have anything to do with it. After a couple of days one of the assistant drillers realised that he could get the American driller to tick the "He is competent" box for a number of the tasks which he routinely performed.

When the next crew took over somebody noticed that the boxes had been filled in and suddenly the floodgates opened. Every time a job was done one of the crew was showing someone else how to do it, and the American drillers found that they did not have to shout and scream at the crew any more. The crew were taking over.

The American drillers found that now they did have time for explanations and the crew were demanding them.

I did one more trip on that rig and was looking forward to returning to work with an increasingly empowered and enthusiastic workforce, a workforce who had taken responsibility for themselves.

Unfortunately real life prevailed and having failed to find sufficient oil in the Orinoco, the rig was shut down.

After the incident the crews demanded ownership of their jobs. It had been very amusing winding up the Americans but what they really wanted was respect and responsibility.

It was not the Americans' fault that they treated the crews this way. All of their working lives this was the only way they had ever seen a drilling team treated, therefore without any other model this was the only way they knew to run their teams.

The turning point came when they were able to appreciate the more immediate cost of management by shouting. It reminded me of my conversation with Paul in "Killer Whales, KPIs and Consequences" in which I was able to put a theoretical price of nine hundred and fifty thousand pounds on the cost of a bollocking.

In this instance I knew that if the driller had not shouted at the logger the mud which was pumped during those fifteen minutes would have been saved. The cost of shouting at the logger was two hundred thousand dollars!

It was easy for the American driller to blame the mud logger for not being more forceful but he did come to realise that here was 'cause and effect'. He as the team leader was the cause and the mud logger's behaviour was the effect.

It would be nice to believe that the crews, including the American drillers, went away with lessons which they could take with them to their next jobs. It takes a lot of practice and support to replace years of conditioning and I knew that it would take more than a single lesson to make a difference

Backword

These stories have been told about the experiences of a number of people, about what they did and felt when the conditions were created to allow them to take ownership. It is clear from this narrative that we can derive the following conclusions :

Stop telling people what to do. People hate being told what to do. It is human nature to avoid doing what we have been told. At the same time we will pretend that we have done what we were told simply to get the boss off our back. The boss is happy because he thinks that we are doing what we were told. We are happy because we are undermining our boss.

Instead **Find out what people want and give it to them**, or give them the reason why they can't have it. Both answers are equally valuable because they both let the individuals know that their opinion has been listened to and is valued. That gives people huge respect.

Don't annoy people. If you do, work out why and learn how not to do it.

Expect to wait for results. There is no magic button you can push that will change behaviour. Trying to push people towards ownership will only increase their resistance to it. If you push for results it will compromise the ownership process and without ownership there can be no results. Be patient, the performance will come when it is ready and you will be amazed.

Recognise achievement. Always look for opportunities to recognise peoples' achievements. In the worst most depressing under performing team there will always be something to praise. Once people feel praised they begin to look for ways of getting more and that means they will start to do the right things. Pavlov was right: if you create an expectation people will respond to it.

Foster pride whenever possible. Recognise people, publish results, tell others about the achievements of your team. Ask others to recognise your team. Pride is a powerful thing. Once people have experienced pride they invariably want more. People achieve more when their efforts are

149

recognised. When they become used to feeling proud they can start to feel ownership. Help them to find their pride.

Encourage Openness. You can't ask people to be open, but you can very easily stop them from being open by the way you behave. If you are rude or curt or patronising, people will not be open. When they speak to you it is your responsibility to make that conversation a positive experience for them, then they will become open with you.

The worst managers believe that they are wonderful because when they ask their team for an opinion they get the response they expect. The workforce do this because they know that the easiest way to get a bad manager to shut up and get off their backs, is to tell him he is wonderful and agree with whatever he says.

Most people who claim to have an open door policy leave the door physically open on the understanding that anybody who enters has to have a very good reason for doing so. This is not an open door. Make sure that you give a positive experience to everybody who comes to speak to you, which means they will look forward to speaking to you next time. That is an open door.

Accept and support ideas/opinions whenever possible. Just because someone has a different way of doing things, it does not mean they are wrong, merely different. Encourage and develop these differences which will introduce a whole different perception.

Be humble. Our function is to create the conditions which allow ownership. Never assume that you know all the answers; if you give the answer to a technical question you stand a good chance of being wrong.

If you are right it will rob someone else of the ownership of finding the solution and will achieve nothing. Try not to look good. Be humble. Help other people find their own answers.

Don't annoy people. This is so important it has to be said twice. If you do annoy someone, try to figure out why and learn from it. If you can't then call someone else to try to work out what happened.

These stories demonstrate the amazing performances achieved when people are allowed to take ownership, and the sustained nature of the changes when they do.

These experiences, which are *Breaking The Mould*, have been documented and developed into a performance improvement process which is easily adapted to any work-place situation, be it on the shop floor, in the office or at home.

Stop telling people what to do. Ask them what you can do to help instead.

Glossary

This book leans on Peters experience gained working in the Oil Drilling industry. Having said that, the lessons that we take away from this book are not lessons on how to improve the oil industry.

The lessons we learn from Peters experience are about people and how to allow them to improve their own performance.

In these stories the improvements occurred in the drilling industry but the real power of this book lies in the fact that these improvements are available to anyone in any industry in any sector.

We are not kidding.

South America

In the text there are a number of places and terms with which the reader may not be familiar. Some of these terms are specific to the drilling industry.

An explanation of these terms will help the reader to a better understanding of the words used in this book and is not intended to explain in any detail the actual drilling operation.

The places are brought to the readers' attention in order to bring some life to what might otherwise be just another set of exotic place names.

Venezuela

Caracas

Caracas is the Capital City of Venezuela.

It lies about 10 miles inland from a point approximately mid way along the Northern Coast of Venezuela.

The city lies in a narrow valley running East-West at an altitude of 3,000 metres between the precipitous mountains that flank it.

Glossary

The city developed slowly from its beginnings in the 17th Century.

Its development was dogged from the beginning by attacks from pirates and earthquakes.

In 1900 there was a severe earthquake which almost completely razed the city but building was recommenced and by the Second World War it had become a booming metropolis.

As the oil, on which Venezuela seems to float, was exploited Caracas continued to grow and in the boom years of the seventies sprouted huge skyscrapers.

In the eighties and nineties the country experienced an equally dramatic economic decline and now the corrugated iron shanty towns of the capital's poor reach high up the steep hillsides to look down on the Skyscrapers at its centre.

The large numbers of people who exist in Caracas without any form of welfare make the city a dangerous place to be. Kidnappings are common, as is theft and armed robbery.

We were assured that a popular diversion for the local population was to wait at the traffic lights with a gun. When the lights turned red and a car stopped the door would be torn open, the occupants ejected and the car stolen. It did not seem to matter a great deal whether or not the driver was shot in the process.

Perhaps this was the reason that traffic lights and other road signs in Venezuela were treated with a slightly looser interpretation than we might be used to. They seemed to be more for advice than in any expectation of strict or literal interpretation.

The taxis drivers advised us to lock the doors and keep the windows up at all times.

I was staying at the Hilton Hotel in the centre of Caracas between flights. I went up to the roof garden for a beer and a bite to eat. I was prepared to be stunned by the astonishing view and was looking forward to the cool tropical evening breeze as I sipped my chilled Polar. I have to say at this point that Polar is Venezuela's best beer. Served to perfection with tiny ice crystals just beginning to grow in the bottom of the bottle. After a hard day at the office you can't beat it.

I was rather surprised when I stepped out of the lift and found a fifteen foot high wall surrounding the roof garden that not only made it impossible to see any view but also cut off the cooling breeze. I was horrified to find that at altitude, in this tropical paradise, the only breeze was provided by a battery of electric fans.

I felt cheated of my view, but my glass of Polar was not going to be denied.

I sat down and rolling the cold glass in my hands stared at the brickwork, trying to imagine the view that I was missing. I was wondering who could have been so crass to put that wall around the garden.

Then the first shots rang out.

They came from the North side of the Hotel, towards the city, about four in number fired together in a group quite quickly. In the space of a few minutes there was another outbreak to the South. This time two guns were involved.

The shooting started with the deeper boom of a large calibre gun followed by the almost impudent popping crack of a much smaller weapon.

This continued sporadically for about two minutes then stopped for long enough to realise that the wall was probably a very good thing to have between me and the evening's entertainment. The same two weapons started up again briefly at some distance to the South and then I didn't hear them again.

While I sat in the roof garden for a little over an hour on that warm evening I counted six different groups of gunfire all coming from different points of the compass. I left fully appreciating the reason that the view and the breeze had been bricked out of existence in favour of the increased probability that the number of customers leaving the garden would be equal to those who had entered.

Maracaibo

Maracaibo is both the name of a city and of the lake on whose shore the city rests. In this book we are more concerned with the Lake.

The Maracaibo Lake sits in the West of Venezuela like a large teardrop 100 miles long. Its Northern tip is connected to the Caribbean by a dredged deepwater channel.

Since 1938, oil has been produced from underneath the lake by platforms that sit on legs on its shallow bottom. The oil is exported by tankers using the channel to get out of the Lake into the Caribbean.

Currently approximately one fifth of the worlds oil production comes from Venezuela and most of that comes from the Maracaibo Lake. The Lake is populated with a large number of oil rigs and a small indigenous population that lives on the fringes of the Lake in huts, also built out over the water on stilts.

Due to the huge amount of oil that has been produced from the lake in its 70 year production history the centre of the Oil industry in Venezuela is understandably in Maracaibo.

For exactly the same reason Maracaibo is a very bleak and tired place to visit.

Maturin

Maturin is the Capital of the Venezuelan state of Monogas.

The city lies about three hundred miles East of Caracas and fifty miles inland from the Caribbean coast.

Maturin is the Oil Capital of the East of Venezuela and developed from the cultured colonial city that it was before the exploitation of the oil began. It is now an untidy sprawling mix of Oil industry hardware outlets and the bars that are necessary to lubricate the acolytes of that industry.

Maturin airport was the last stop before the journey that took us further East out to the Delta of the Orinoco River.

Rio Orinoco

The Orinoco is one of the most significant rivers in South America. It rises West of Venezuela in the mountains at the Northern end of the Andes in Colombia.

The river sweeps Eastwards bisecting Venezuela for over 1,500 miles until it empties into the Caribbean at a point directly South of Trinidad.

As the river approaches the coast it fans out into an enormous delta that covers an area of over 8,000 square miles. It is the oil bearing sands beneath this delta that are beginning to hold the interest of the oil industry.

Travel round the Delta more recently is by air. On the ground the tangled mess of mangroves ensures that the only way to travel is by water.

Pedernales

Pedernales is a tiny village of indigenous Warao Indians at the mouth of the Orinoco Delta. Their principal occupation, using traditional Lanchas, is fishing.

The village today has not changed a great deal but around it has grown the infrastructure to service the oil reserves in the Delta. Maybe the reserves have proved less than anticipated or perhaps the industry is beginning to be a little more sensitive to the lives of the local population.

For whatever reason, the village retains its charm with little of the intrusion that has coloured the way that the oil industry has treated other parts of Venezuela.

158

El Tigre

El Tigre was a small town of little significance until the discovery of the new oil reserves in the centre of Venezuela. It is very much in the frontier town stage of development. There is little in the way of infrastructure other than the numerous Hotels, bars and ubiquitous suppliers of equipment to the oilfield.

It was in El Tigre that the Rig Manager, Willie Schmidt, lived and from there ran the Drilling Rig that is the subject of the first eight chapters of this book.

Merida

The city of Merida sits high in the Venezuelan Andes at an altitude of over a mile.

The altitude even this close to the equator makes for an ideal climate. Warm during the day but cool enough to sleep well in the evening. The city is home to the second largest university in Venezuela, the Universidad de Los Andes.

Although only a hundred and twenty miles South of Maracaibo Lake, Merida's remoteness and therefore relative isolation means that the city has retained its full colonial splendour without being compromised too much by the glass and steel of the new industry that has scarred so much of the rest of Venezuela.

Merida has been called the Oxford of Venezuela. It seems to exist on a plane above the rest of Venezuela.

This has more to do with stability, innocent industry and a pride in its colonial history than actual altitude.

Puerto La Cruz (Port or Haven of the Cross)

Puerto La Cruz was founded in 1671 as the colonial capital for Anzoategui State.

It suffered in the war of independence in 1811 when Simon Bolivar defended the city It is still filled with superb examples of colonial architecture.

Puerto La Cruz is now a busy South American Town whose prosperity comes from two sources. The first is the huge refinery at Guaraguao (Pronounced Warowow) through which all of the substantial oil exports from the East of Venezuela flow.

The second is the tourist industry which serves the many thousands of people who flock to the innumerable beautiful beaches and offshore islands every weekend.

The industry serves the tourist at all levels. From the families who hire sun umbrellas on the islands and spend the day eating shellfish and drinking beer bought from the vendors who walk the beaches, to the visitors from further afield who store their power boats on shelves, stacked ten high in huge warehouses. There is not enough room to keep them all on the water at the same time.

At the last count there were over 50,000 registered power boats stored in Puerto La Cruz.

For all this prosperity, if you go down to the beaches during the week you will find them busy with "Los Pobres". These are the families from the shanty towns for whom the beaches are free on weekdays, but for whom access is denied at the weekend.

The Yukon Quest

The Yukon Quest mentioned in Chapter nine is the route of a sled dog race from Whitehorse to Fairbanks in Alaska. In alternate years it is run in the opposite direction.

The trail is 1,000 miles long and follows the old Gold Rush routes of the 1800's.

It takes two weeks or more to travel the trail with only the very best looking for a time of ten days or less to be in with a chance of winning.

The Iditarod

The Iditarod is known as the last great race on Earth. It is also the longest sled race at 1,151 miles. It is run over the trail from Anchorage to Nome and first took place in 1973. The first winner took nearly three weeks to complete the course but today's competitors are covering the same distance in nine days.

The event was ostensibly to celebrate the sled runs made in 1925 when a diphtheria epidemic struck Nome. The town was completely frozen in and the only way that medicine could be brought in was by dog sled. 18 teams made the trip with the medicine that saved the community. The dogs became heroes and one of them, Balto, is commemorated by a statue raised to his memory in Central Park, New York.

I used the word 'ostensibly' because the real reason the race was started was to celebrate and maintain a culture that was beginning to be lost. As the distances in Alaska were progressively being shrunk by trains, planes and snowmobiles, people began to realise that unless something was done the sled dog as a breed would be consigned to history and a few scratchy black and white films.

Today the race continues annually.

Glossary of Drilling Terms

The Rig

The Rig is the generic term for all of the equipment needed to drill an oil well.

The Well

Sometimes known as the hole.

The well is the physical hole that is drilled in the ground from the surface to the oil producing layers. In the past the well was drilled straight down, or in whatever direction it chose until the oil bearing formation was reached.

There was no control over the direction the well took.

Today we can not only continuously monitor the direction the well is drilled using gyros carried in the drill pipe behind the bit, we can also steer the drill in the direction that we want the well to go. This allows us to start drilling the well vertically, and in Willie Schmidt's case, to turn the well gradually to the horizontal.

By the time Willie's wells reached a vertical depth of 1,000ft the hole was being drilled horizontally and continued so for the next 5,000 feet.

The reason for this in Willie's case was that the oil producing layer was very thin and the oil very thick and therefore slow moving. By drilling a long horizontal hole through the producing layer the total amount of oil that seeped into the well over that length was sufficient to make drilling the well economic.

In the North Sea the oil is much lighter and flows very easily but in most cases the production zones directly beneath the fixed oil rigs have already been depleted.

In this case directional drilling is used to aim the well at new production zones that could be as much as six miles away from the rig.

The Drill Bit

There are two principal types of drill bit whose use depends on the type of formation and the well that is being drilled.

The PCD bit and the Roller Cone bit.

The analogy is the difference between a bit we would use for wood and the one we use for masonry. These two types of bit are for different types of masonry.

The Derrick

The most obvious part of the rig is the derrick.

The derrick sits over the well and can be over 30m high. The Top Drive motor used to drill the well runs up and down in the derrick, it is also used to store the drill pipe.

The Top Drive

When the well is drilled the drill bit advances through the formation .The drill bit is turned by a large electric or hydraulic motor called the Top Drive which is suspended in the derrick and is connected to the drill bit by the drill pipe.

As the drill bit advances through the formation the Top Drive, which starts at the top of the derrick, slowly descends.

When it reaches the bottom drilling stops and the Top Drive is pulled back to the top of the derrick.

A new section of drill pipe is added and the drilling operation can start again.

This operation to add new lengths of drill pipe is repeated until the well reaches its designed depth.

The Top Drive Grabber

On some, but not all, Top Drives there is a hydraulic clamp which is used to grip the drill pipe, this then rotates the pipe to screw one joint into the next.

The grabber has gripping dies made of extremely hard, but brittle, material. These dies are designed to bite into the drill pipe and therefore grip it.

Drill string

This is the expression for the total length of the drill pipe from the Top Drive all the way down to the drill bit.

Drill Pipe

This is the link between the Top Drive motor and the drill bit.

Drill pipe is supplied in joints. Each joint is 30 feet long but in larger rigs three joints are screwed together to make 'a stand' of 90 feet. Each time drilling stops to add more pipe, drilling time is lost.

It is therefore more efficient to add a 90ft stand of drill pipe (3 Joints) to the drill string than it is a single 30 foot joint.

By screwing many stands together wells can be drilled for considerable distances.

The primary function of the pipe is to transfer the torque from the Top Drive motor to the drill bit. Since most oil wells these days are drilled away from the vertical the drill pipe lies on the low side of the hole.

As the pipe is rotated the joints of the pipe are worn away by their contact with the walls of the well. In order to protect the joints they have bands of hard steel set into them. When the pipe rotates in contact with the rock these hard bands prevent the pipe joint being eroded.

Tripping pipe

Tripping pipe is the expression used when the bit is being retrieved to the surface or a new one is being run into an already drilled hole. This operation consists of screwing or unscrewing pipe then running into or out of the hole and repeating the operation until the old bit is retrieved or the new bit has reached the point where drilling stopped.

Whole days are spent in this manner tripping pipe.

Slips

When tripping pipe out of the well the Top Drive is raised to the top of the derrick so that a stand of pipe is exposed in the derrick. Before the stand can be unscrewed the drill string has to be supported, otherwise there would be nothing to prevent the remainder of the string from falling down the well.

This is done by placing the slips around the pipe at the rig floor. The profile of the slips is a wedge shape. When the driller lowers the drill string the slips jam the pipe in the well bore and allow the exposed stand to be unscrewed.

The slips are released when the top drive takes the weight of the drill string and they are removed until another stand is due to be added or removed.

Laying out pipe

When it is necessary to pull the drill pipe out of the well the joints of pipe are taken into the derrick where they are unscrewed. If the well has reached its design depth the drill pipe will be 'Laid Out' on the pipe deck to leave the derrick clear for the next operation, running casing.

If the well is not complete and is going to require more drilling the drill pipe will be stacked in the derrick in the 'Set Back Area' where it will be available when drilling operations recommence.

Drilling Mud

As the bit gouges away the rock, drilling mud is blasted at high pressure through the bit to wash the cuttings created away from the bit and back up to the surface. If this did not happen the cuttings would remain at the bottom of the well and clog up the bit.

The Drill Pipe is hollow

During drilling the mud is pumped down through the centre of the drill pipe to the drill bit. This mud has a number of functions among them lubricating and cooling the bit. As the well is drilled tremendous forces are created at the cutting head. To preserve the bit it must be lubricated and prevented from overheating.

When the drill bit advances it creates cuttings at the face of the hole. Unlike a wood drill that generates a spiral of cut wood which comes out of the hole on its own, the rock drill creates discrete cuttings that need to be transported back to the surface.

The mud has to be thick enough to carry these cuttings from the drill bit between the drill pipe and the wall of the well back up to the surface.

Once the mud is on the surface it is run over vibrating screens called Shakers.

The shakers allow the mud to fall through a mesh and the cuttings, which may be anything from fine sand to coarse gravel chips, are gathered from the Shakers and shipped off to be used as landfill or otherwise disposed of.

The drilling mud maintains the pressure at the bottom of the well. If there was no mud in the well then the air pressure at the bottom of the well would be atmospheric pressure at that depth.

At the same depth the pressure of the formation would be much greater due to the weight of all the formation above it. This would cause the walls of the well to burst inwards, filling the well bore and making drilling impossible.

The weight of the mud is adjusted by adding or removing heavy solids. This is done by a contractor called the Mud Engineer. He does this to stop the walls of the well from caving in and to optimise the other functions of the mud.

The weight of the mud has the additional effect of increasing the pressure in the well making it less likely that gas, oil or water will be able to force its way into the well and cause a blow-out.

This is particularly important in the case of gas.

If a bubble gets into the well bore it will start to rise and as it rises it will expand.

As it expands it rises faster and as it rises faster it expands faster. When an uncontrolled gas bubble hits the surface it can be travelling very quickly and can devastate the rig.

Rapidly rising gas bubbles have been known to throw the entire length of the drill pipe out of the well. If that happens you can be fairly sure you are not having a good day. If the gas bubble subsequently ignites then you are definitely having a bad day.

Casing

Casing or Liner is put into the well after the design depth is reached.

The casing is a steel tube supplied in Joints 30 feet long which screw together in much the same way that the drill pipe does.

The purpose of the casing is to support the walls of the well such that they do not collapse inwards and impeded production. Once in the well the casing stays in place throughout the life of the well.

If an obstacle is encountered when running the casing it may be necessary to pull it out or effectively, to trip the casing. This is an expensive problem should it occur and the solution normally involves re-running the drilling assembly to remove the obstacle.

Cementing

When casing has been run it is necessary to cement it into place. To do this liquid cement is made up and then pumped down the well in a slug to the place it is required.

The cement is a complex chemical cocktail of inhibitors and accelerators depending on the function it is designed for and how long it will take to pump it into place.

On occasion the chemical cocktail can be wrong or the placing of the slug may be delayed. When this happens and the cement sets in a place it is not wanted the results can be devastating.

Cementing is a regular part of the engineering of a well and there is normally a contractor on board with permanent responsibility for the cementing operations.

Rig Skid

In any drilling operation we can only drill one hole from one position. If we want to drill another well we have to change the position that we start from.

The operation to change the start position is called 'Skidding the Rig'. The rig has no wheels and is therefore physically slid or skidded from one position to another with large hydraulic jacks. The distance skidded varies depending on the type of operation.

Offshore the distance can vary from a few metres to fifty or more. In onshore drilling the distance of each skid is more likely to be consistent at around 15m – there will always be exceptions.

Rig Move

In this operation all of the wells required in a particular location have been drilled.

To continue drilling, the rig has to be packed up and physically moved from one geographical location to the next.

Offshore this means dismantling the rig and moving it by barge to a new location.

This operation is carried out infrequently.

In the onshore operation it may happen as often as every few months. The whole rig will be dismantled and loaded on trucks to be driven to the new location where it is reassembled.

In remote locations, such as central Venezuela, when the Oilfield is first surveyed the road network required to exploit the field will be one of the first pieces of infrastructure installed.

Rig Manager

This is a man who is not normally resident on the rig. It is his job to deal with all of the functions that don't actually involve drilling. He is the man who arranges the supply of all the equipment, the stores and personnel that the rig needs to drill the well.

Country Manager

In Venezuela the drilling contractor had six rigs working in the country. Each of these rigs had a manager but the overall responsibility for all of the contractor operations in the country belonged to this man.

Toolpusher

The Toolpusher is the man who is resident on the rig and is the senior member of the Drill Crew. His job is the day to day drilling of the well.

This used to be a hands on job but is becoming more of an administrative nightmare. The Toolpusher is normally promoted from the rig crew on the basis of his work as a driller.

He is then expected to perform equally effectively as an administrator.

Driller

At any one time on an offshore platform there are two drilling teams, one dayshift and one on nights. In charge of each of these teams is the Driller who in turn reports to the Toolpusher.

The Driller is the man who actually drills the well. He is in control of the drill bit and is responsible for the speed of rotation, the weight that is put on the bit and cleaning the cuttings out of The Well.

Derrickman

This is the member of the crew who works at the top of the derrick.

His job is to stow and remove the drill pipe from the derrick where it is kept when drilling or tripping pipe.

Roughneck

There are normally four or five Roughnecks in the crew.

These are the men who work on the Rig Floor handling the Drill Pipe and the Slips.

The Driller directs their operations.

Roustabouts

These are the crew members who work on the pipe deck.

The pipe deck is a stowage area remote from the derrick where drill pipe, liner and other equipment is laid down when not in use.

The Roustabout's job is to move the drill pipe, casing or any other equipment that is required, between the pipe deck and the drill floor.

Glossary

Toolbox Talk

At significant intervals in the drilling operation the crew will get together as a group with the Toolpusher and have a toolbox talk. This normally occurs when one operation has finished and another is about to begin. The Toolbox talk is the occasion when the Toolpusher explains to the Drill Crew what the next part of the drilling operation entails and what they are expected to do.

Las Charlas

Literally translated Charla means a chat.

In South America this was the period of 15 minutes every shift before the new crew went on to the rig. Everybody ready to start work would gather in the tea shack to listen to one of the off going crew explain what they had done for the previous shift, where they had got to in the programme and what operations the new crew could expect to see in the next 8 hours. This period of 15 minutes before the crew went on shift became the opportunity each day to find out from the crews what they needed to do their jobs and give them feedback for their ideas.

There is a similar period at the beginning of every shift on drilling rigs everywhere but in South America the Charlas became a place for reflection on the lessons that had been learned and a forum for the collection of new ideas and planning strategies.

This forum and the way it was run became key in generating the environment from which the crews were able to take ownership of the operation.

The Charlas became a very important part of the process that allowed the crews to become powerful by taking ownership of their own operations.

About the Author

Peter Hunter's career started on a nautical theme. After leaving school he spent six years as a navigating officer in the Merchant Navy working within a strict hierarchy It was not until he joined the Royal Navy in 1988 that he began to realise how valuable people really were when they were allowed to be.

Peter studied for his masters degree at Cranfield Institute of Technology before going to Britannia Royal Naval College, Dartmouth as an Instructor Officer, Royal Navy. He rose to become Head of Department at the RN Strategic Systems School, Faslane where he further developed the concept that "management is a two way thing". After 8 years with other consultancies Peter formed his own management consulting agency in Portincaple on the West Coast of Scotland.

Hunter Business Consultancy associates are now based all over the United Kingdom and are expanding into Europe. The specific aim is to make those "Breaking The Mould" skills and techniques, that have served the Corporate world so well available to ordinary businessmen and their management process.

The "Breaking the Mould" performance improvement process has been developed from the lessons and examples detailed in this book. Details of how to implement the process in your own organisation or book a place on a "Breaking the Mould" Seminar can be found on the website at :

www.breakingthemould.co.uk and at **www.hunter-consultants.co.uk.**

The "Breaking the Mould" process is available worldwide.

173